PRAISE FOR THE WO.
MARY PIPHER

SEEKING PEACE

"Like the oldest child and doctor's daughter she is, she shares her falling apart and coming back together in order to help others who, as she was, may be in silent crisis. This is a generous book conceived and executed by a compassionate and unquiet mind. She is no paragon, just another soul on the common march between birth and death."

—*Publishers Weekly* (starred review)

"This is an insightful and terribly personal memoir of an active and successful life, and of how her almost desperate need for inner peace amid the noise of her world has dominated so many of her days."

—*Lincoln Journal Star*

"The perfect book for anyone striving to soothe an agitated mind."

—*Body & Soul*

"Pipher's account of being 'the worst Buddhist in the world'—driven, anxious, self-blaming—is hard to put down with its smooth, compact, and insightful prose. . . . An absorbing chronicle of discovery."

—*Booklist*

WRITING TO CHANGE THE WORLD

"[Pipher] offers useful advice . . . [This] will encourage idealistic inspiring writers, who will surely find inspiration in her assertion that writing can change the world." —*Publishers Weekly*

REVIVING OPHELIA

"An important book . . . Pipher shines high-beam headlights on the world of teenage girls." —*Los Angeles Times*

ANOTHER COUNTRY

"Totally accessible . . . A compassionate . . . look at the disconnect between baby boomers and their aging parents or grandparents." —*USA Today*

THE SHELTER OF EACH OTHER

"A canny mix of optimism and practicality gives Pipher's fans a way to resist the worst of the culture around them and substitute the best of themselves." —*Newsweek*

ALSO BY MARY PIPHER

Writing to Change the World (2006)

Letters to a Young Therapist (2003)

*The Middle of Everywhere: Helping Refugees
Enter the American Community* (2002)

*Another Country: Navigating the Emotional
Terrain of Our Elders* (2000)

*Hunger Pains: The Modern Woman's
Tragic Quest For Thinness* (1997)

*The Shelter of Each Other:
Rebuilding Our Families* (1996)

*Reviving Ophelia: Saving the Selves
of Adolescent Girls* (1994)

SEEKING
PEACE

Chronicles of the

Worst Buddhist

in the World

MARY PIPHER

RIVERHEAD BOOKS

New York

RIVERHEAD BOOKS
Published by the Penguin Group
Penguin Group (USA) Inc.
375 Hudson Street, New York, New York 10014, USA
Penguin Group (Canada), 90 Eglinton Avenue East, Suite 700, Toronto, Ontario M4P 2Y3, Canada
(a division of Pearson Penguin Canada Inc.)
Penguin Books Ltd., 80 Strand, London WC2R 0RL, England
Penguin Group Ireland, 25 St. Stephen's Green, Dublin 2, Ireland (a division of Penguin Books Ltd.)
Penguin Group (Australia), 250 Camberwell Road, Camberwell, Victoria 3124, Australia
(a division of Pearson Australia Group Pty. Ltd.)
Penguin Books India Pvt. Ltd., 11 Community Centre, Panchsheel Park, New Delhi—110 017, India
Penguin Group (NZ), 67 Apollo Drive, Rosedale, North Shore 0632, New Zealand
(a division of Pearson New Zealand Ltd.)
Penguin Books (South Africa) (Pty.) Ltd., 24 Sturdee Avenue, Rosebank, Johannesburg 2196,
South Africa

Penguin Books Ltd., Registered Offices: 80 Strand, London WC2R 0RL, England

The publisher does not have any control over and does not assume any responsibility for author or third-party
websites or their content.

Copyright © 2009 Mary Pipher
Cover design © 2009 Abby Weintraub
Cover photograph © John Elk III / Lonely Planet Images
Book design by Meighan Cavanaugh

All rights reserved.
No part of this book may be reproduced, scanned, or distributed in any printed or electronic form without
permission. Please do not participate in or encourage piracy of copyrighted materials in violation of the au-
thor's rights. Purchase only authorized editions.
RIVERHEAD is a registered trademark of Penguin Group (USA) Inc.
The RIVERHEAD logo is a trademark of Penguin Group (USA) Inc.

First Riverhead hardcover edition: March 2009
First Riverhead trade paperback edition: April 2010
Riverhead trade paperback ISBN: 978-1-59448-440-7

The Library of Congress has catalogued the Riverhead hardcover edition as follows:

Pipher, Mary, Bray.
Seeking peace : chronicles of the worst Buddhist in the world / Mary Pipher
    p. cm.
  ISBN: 978-1-59448-861-0
  1. Pipher, Mary, Bray.   2. Buddhists—Biography.   I. Title
BQ 978.I628A3   2009   2008050337
294.3'092—dc22
  [B]

PRINTED IN THE UNITED STATES OF AMERICA

Penguin is committed to publishing works of quality and integrity. In that spirit, we are proud to offer this
book to our readers; however, the story, the experiences, and the words are the author's alone.

*To my grandparents and
their grandparents' grandparents,
and to my grandchildren and
my grandchildren's grandchildren*

CONTENTS

SECOND LIFETIME

Out of clutter, find simplicity. From discord, find harmony. In the middle of difficulty lies opportunity.

ALBERT EINSTEIN

Life is this simple: We are living in a world that is absolutely transparent and the divine is shining through it all the time.

THOMAS MERTON

PRELUDE

Let me be straight with you. I am not writing this book as an expert on inner peace. Nor am I offering sage advice from one who has been to the mountaintop. My authority does not come from being a relaxed and happy person, but rather from being a person who has sought calmness and happiness all of her life. I address you as a woman who has spent plenty of time talking herself and others down from emotional ledges.

I know about inner peace the way Nelson Mandela knew about freedom when he wrote *Long Walk to Freedom*. He had spent almost his entire adult life in prison on Robben Island, but he struggled every minute of his life to break the chains of his oppression. Since my girlhood, I have yearned for tranquillity. Few people have sought serenity with more ardor or have worked harder at relaxing than I have. (I do note the contradictions of that last sentence.)

The subtitle for this book was inspired by a remark my husband, Jim, made several years ago. One morning after my meditation session, I was racing around the house, stressed and spaced

out. After noticing my whirlwind of commotion, Jim said, some-
what jokingly, "You are the worst Buddhist in the world." His
words stopped me in my tracks. They hurt my feelings and irritated me. But later, I saw their ironic potential.

Any student of Buddhism knows that we are all the Buddha
waiting to manifest our glorious being. Jim's conceptualization of
"the worst Buddhist" is simply not possible. Yet there is a sense in
which he is absolutely right. I may well be the least suitable can-
didate for Buddhism on the planet. I am an efficiency expert, a
worrier, and—to put it charitably—scattered. When I begin tasks
A, B, and C, I end up doing A, X, J, Z, B, D, Q, W, and, if I am
lucky, I eventually find my way back to C.

While my laid-back, slow-talking husband finishes a sentence,
my mind jogs three laps around town and generates a dozen new
observations and plans. Once when Jim was telling me something,
I said, "I have a thought about that, no, two actually, no, I mean
three, well, really seven." I wasn't kidding. Once, when I started a
sentence to my son with the words "I have a theory," Zeke inter-
rupted me to remark, "Mom, you have a theory about everything."

I can see all sides of every issue. From my point of view, the answer
to every question is: "It depends." Every judgment, every decision,
must be put in context. Motive is sometimes as important as results.
The same action—stealing a loaf of bread, for example—may be
labeled common theft or heroism depending on the situation.

Years ago, I coined a term for myself—"omnivalent," an adjec-
tive that describes a person who has complex and changing ideas
about everything all the time. As my daughter, Sara, said, I can
have mixed feelings about a paper clip. I am capable of generating
a hundred judgments per minute. That interview should have

been handled more smoothly. Those flowers are not properly arranged. Or, I should be editing my manuscript instead of watching
that kestrel.

I am phobic about wasting time. I carry a notebook and books
or magazines everywhere, and if I am waiting in line, I read or
make additional to-do lists. I am easily bored, moody, exuberant,
obsessed with sleep and greedy for sensory pleasure, knowledge
and love. I work with three calendars, and I constantly overcom-
mit myself to projects and people.

I remember every argument I've ever had with Jim and every
time in my life that someone hurt my feelings. I am the poster child
for not letting things go. Serenity is my ultimate abstract concept.

Who needs Buddhism more than I do? Who could benefit more
from learning to sit down, breathe slowly and rest the mind? Yet
when I first shared my interest in meditation with friends, I received
befuddled reactions. "That doesn't seem like you." Or, "Slowing
down your brain? Impossible." Or even worse, "Given the way your
mind works, I am not sure you should try something like that."

I would not describe myself as a Buddhist, but rather as "Bud-
dhish." I have only a cursory knowledge of Buddhism's history and
its different forms. I do not have a teacher, and I don't identify
with a particular school. I wouldn't presume to proselytize my version of Buddhism Lite, but in this book I hope to demonstrate how
reading about Buddhism and learning meditation skills have been
useful to me.

I will make no distinction between mindfulness training and
Buddhist meditation. "Mindfulness training" is a Western term
for Buddhist practices that have been adapted for all kinds of settings. Buddhists talk about "breaking attachments" and "taming

the monkey mind." Mindfulness therapists are more likely to speak of being present in the moment and of fully experiencing one's life. However, they embrace similar skills: calming down, practicing patience and self-discipline, facing life honestly, tolerating distress and discomfort, suspending judgment of self and others, and opening to joy. The goals are similar as well: inner peace, self-acceptance and a sense of connection with all life.

Until I started meditating in my fifties, I had never, not even for ten seconds, done nothing. I have rushed through much of my life as if I were late for an appointment. I have spent decades ruminating about the past and the future while skipping over the present moment. Even now, when I meditate, I'm tempted to set the timer on twenty-nine minutes, instead of thirty.

One of the most comforting aspects of my study of Buddhism has been learning that others also have a great deal of trouble controlling their minds during meditation. I have encountered many people who also believe they are the worst Buddhists in the world and that their brains are uniquely busy. Often they think, as I did, that their genetics and history have left them especially cursed. Just as I want to be happy and free of suffering, so, it turns out, does everyone else. This simple notion has helped me accept my own foibles and feel compassion for those of others.

I was first attracted to Buddhism not as a religion, but as a way to calm down. I would argue that the Buddha is the world's most ancient and brilliant psychologist. From my perspective, his teachings contain highly sophisticated formulations for mental and spiritual health. They cover a vast range of topics, from how to relate to others to how to prepare for death. In many ways, Sigmund Freud and the Buddha taught the same lessons. Freud said that neurosis is the refusal to experience one's own suffering. The

Buddha said that in order to be free, one must accept, even embrace, suffering.

For as long as I can remember, I've had a turbulent inner life. Because I constantly experience a nearly overwhelming rush of thoughts and emotions, I have learned to keep most of them to myself. However, I am also a gregarious person who likes to be helpful. When Kate, my six-year-old granddaughter, prays for goodness, she reminds me of myself. We both like to be in the thick of the action, doing for others.

I always have been more prone to dreaminess and more intense than most people. As a girl, when I hung up clothes to dry, I made up stories about each pair of socks and underpants. I married the towels to each other and deemed the washcloths their children, to whom I assigned names, ages and personalities.

I am also subject to despair. Deep in my heart I have believed myself to be unlovable and my mistakes to be unforgivable. I have fought and mostly lost battles with insomnia. Since high school, when I read Truman Capote's *In Cold Blood*, I have wasted many a night in bed worrying about everything from being murdered, to never having a boyfriend, to nuclear holocaust.

Most mornings I wake up curious and eager to see what will happen next. I have always yearned for new experiences and new ways of looking at the world. Yet all this energy has a down side. I can always find more work to do, more books to read, more projects to take on, more adventures to schedule, more people to enjoy and, perhaps most frustrating, more ways to improve myself.

Psychologists make a distinction between "satisficers" and maximizers. Satisficers are able to accept much of life as "good enough." Maximizers always wish things were a little bit better. My aunt Grace, a satisficer, said, "I get what I want, but I know what to want."

I have been the quintessential maximizer. The phrase "greener pastures" could have been coined for me. My friend Randy jokes that even when I am enjoying myself, I will suggest, "Let's do something else that might make us even happier." At a restaurant with a friend, I'll think, "My halibut is great, but her eggplant Parmesan looks tastier." Or, "Jim would be an even better husband if he would let me read him poetry." Or, "This mountaintop is fantastic, but that one to the south has an even prettier view."

Being a seeker is both a gift and a burden. For me, the burden is the sense of guilt that I am not sufficiently kind, good and useful. These last few years I've even chastised myself for not experiencing enough rapture. I could form a support group for people who try too hard.

Embedded in the concept "seeker" is the less flattering word "dissatisfied." Japanese poet Basho wrote, "Even in Kyoto, I yearn for Kyoto."

Yet the gift of seeking is growth. Seekers are as propelled by zest and curiosity as they are by yearning. Throughout history, seekers have been world travelers, inventors, artists, poets, scientists and philosophers.

The Buddha was a seeker who left his home to spend years in the wilderness, resisting sleep, denying himself food, mortifying his flesh and meditating constantly. Under a Bodhi tree, he experienced his great insight that suffering ends when we stop striving to control life and accept whatever comes next with compassion and awareness. His teaching became: "Stop seeking. Be here now." He must have found the results of his enlightenment to be slightly paradoxical. I can identify with that.

INTRODUCTION

This book is a quest describing a quest. It is the story of a little girl who struggles to be happy in a childhood filled with love, abandonment, turmoil and loneliness. She grows up, raises two children, and lives as most Americans do. Then she is catapulted into a life she neither anticipated nor desired. She has her hour in the sun, despairs and crashes back to earth. She reorients herself and recrafts her life.

The narrative is uniquely my own. I am the only girl born, in 1947, to Frank and Avis Bray, parents who served fried rattlesnake, poke salad and field corn for dinner and who never spent a minute indoors if they could help it. Only I, at six years old, lived for a year without my mother in a trailer behind my uncle Otis's house two miles from Sparta, Missouri. Only this Mary lived in Beaver City in 1959 and spent lazy afternoons catching frogs and turtles while her peers fretted about hemlines and lipstick.

Yet the basic map and milestones of my story are universal. We all search for understanding, love and respect. We strive to make sense of ourselves and our environments. Over the course of our lifetimes, we encounter love and loss, success and dismal failure. We establish our characteristic ways of coping with adversity. We search for a way to develop our talents and employ them for the benefit of others. We all seek the holy grail of self-acceptance. We become more and more ourselves, but we remember everyone else.

On my journey I faced certain challenges many times over. I suffered losses and learned to compensate. At moments when I felt most alone, I found loving people. When I was ignorant, I worked to understand what I could. Often I believed I was irredeemable. I endured fright, loneliness and despair, but I carried on. And even as I have been a wanderer, all my life I have searched for home.

In my earliest memories of myself, I have certain characteristics. At age two, I loved people fiercely. I still do. For as long as I can remember, I have been a shy girl with a galloping mind and a lively imagination. I have always considered myself to be competent and resilient. Over time, I have been influenced by circumstance, and yet in some essential ways, I am unchanged. With this book, my quest has been to explore my life in terms of core and periphery, theme and variation.

On every page, I asked myself, "Who am I?" Throughout the writing process, I have reflected on basic questions. What did I inherit from my ancestors? What did I learn from my surroundings? Was I loved? Was I good? Did I matter?

I found the experience of writing about my life to be deeply strengthening. Yet this book caused me more trouble than any other I have written. Writing a book about freeing myself from neurosis—what Buddhists sometimes call "the trance of self"—required, shockingly, a constant focus on myself! Only I could come up with a complicated writing assignment such as: "Explain your efforts to stop trying to stop trying." I have had moments when I wasn't sure whether I was gaining clarity or falling into a cauldron of boiling self-absorption.

Self-study is not for sissies. When I take on a new project, I immerse myself entirely and intensely in the subject. This constant scrutiny worked well when the topic was teenage girls or refugees, but when the subject was myself, it felt claustrophobic. By the time I completed my first draft, I felt I had run an emotional and intellectual marathon. I had learned a great deal, but the process had torn me down. I wrote my editor: "Remind me never to write about myself again. I am weary of me, me, me. My next book will be on something less intense and complicated, like the history of Poland or the inner workings of the Vatican."

There are three kinds of secrets—those we keep from certain people but not others; those we keep from everyone, and those we keep from ourselves. Writing this book forced me to deal with all three. Many formerly private aspects of my life are now public. Even Jim and my children learned new things about me. And as I explored my own life, I was shattered to discover many aspects of my experience I had long avoided.

For most of my life, I have recalled good times and loving moments. When I remembered my girlhood, I painted myself into scenes as a happy, loved girl, filled with honorable intentions. I worked to construct a temple of comforting beliefs—that I was nurtured, respected, and in control. With this quest, I have probed deep layers of memory that I had long struggled to ignore. As I faced the facts and examined painful recollections, I realized that what happened to me is both more unpleasant and more interest-

ing than my previous "official" story. When I finally gave myself
permission to travel with my eyes open, my reactions have been a
clamorous mix of "Hallelujah" and "Ouch."

Writing this book, I confronted numerous problems. How do I
make sense of things that happened to me before I had language?
How much should I trust my memories? What should remain private? Like many members of my generation, I have been around.
I've smoked marijuana, hitchhiked and done countless other things
I would just as soon my grandchildren and my former therapy clients not read about. I still commit most of the seven deadly sins on
a regular basis. I would feel silly telling my story as if I had always
been some pure and prudent person. I am reasonably wholesome
now, but I've had many experiences that directed me toward my
current life. How much of this do I need to disclose to be honest
and yet not write a lurid confessional?

Wright Morris observed that anything processed by memory is
fiction. To the best of my ability, I have made sure that the times,
places and basic facts of my story were accurate, but the narrative
you will read is what I understand about what I remember, a story
built by attention and interpretation.

Huck Finn said of his creator, Mark Twain, that he "told the
truth, mainly." I hope that can be said of me.

Writing about my own family was complicated. I believe that the
way to honor people is to describe them as they actually were. To
gloss over flaws or to invent virtues is to suggest that who people were
wasn't good enough. My relatives can stand on their records. I have
no desire to malign anyone, yet I want to explain what actually happened to me. I don't want to offer up a narrative soaked in Clorox.

Even though my siblings and children are important parts of

my life, I don't write much about them. Through no fault of their own, they have a writer in the family. Their stories are theirs to tell. And even though we all dance around a common flagpole of place, people and time, we weave amid the other dancers with our own ribbons. Our choreography is uniquely our own.

I am also aware of the ridiculousness of trying to explain that being a best-selling writer led me to misery and depression. I know there are a million people out there who would love to be published by a national press or to have any kind of success that led to fame, money and travel. Until this happened to me, I was one of those people.

Convincing people that great success isn't all it's cracked up to be is a hard sell. For a long time, I've been aware of that and, up until now, perhaps wisely, I have kept my mouth shut. I expect many readers would trade places with me in a minute and, indeed, there are people who would enjoy what I found to be extraordinarily difficult. But I am too anxious and self-critical for life on a grand stage.

In this book, I tried to tell my truth, which includes what happened to me as a person after 1994. Yet I can imagine readers feeling slightly bitter as they read of my woes. I can just hear my writer friend Matt saying, "I should be so unlucky!" To those readers, I can only say I hope that your dreams come true and you are able to see for yourself your own reactions. I fervently want you to relish your good fortune.

Until 1994, when *Reviving Ophelia* was published and climbed to number-one on best-seller lists around the country, I led what I considered a balanced life. I was a wife, mother, teacher and therapist. I had the usual adult problems: children's report cards, work

stress, financial worries and, as is the case with almost all working
mothers, limited discretionary time. My mother had died in 1992,
my son had graduated from high school in 1989 and left for college, and my daughter was in her senior year of high school. I felt
a great sense of loss about all these events. But I was happy. My
husband played in local bands, and he and I enjoyed a life filled
with musicians and writers. I spent my free time camping, hiking,
writing and drinking coffee with my friends.

Then, without my really planning on it, I entered a new era. I
said good-bye to my ordinary life and embarked on a more complicated and stressful one. I kept my day jobs, but I also began lectur-
ing all over the world. Within months, I was speaking to large
crowds and conducting daylong workshops for professionals. Members of Congress flew me to D.C. to educate them about teenagers.
The Polish ambassador's wife invited me to a conference in War-
saw. Between 1994 and 2002, I wrote and published four more
books, two of which became best-sellers.

When I traveled to Chicago to be on *Oprah*, my son drove me
to the airport. On the way, Zeke asked me, "Mom, this isn't going to change anything, is it?" I blithely reassured him that it
wouldn't. At the time, I had no idea how much would change and
how quickly. My success as an author had triggered a process as
dramatic and irreversible as the push of a boulder that starts an
avalanche.

Leaving my life as a relatively contented person behind, I entered a zone of constant pressure, scrutiny and high stakes. My
schedule, which had been manageable, became frenetic and not
entirely under my control. I was bombarded with invitations and
requests from people I didn't know. As my familiar world slipped
away, the Mary I had known for forty-seven years vanished as

well. I hadn't made conscious choices about any of this; it just happened. No one was more surprised than I was.

By 2002, my identity had exceeded its shelf life and many of
my certainties turned stale. I had always considered myself competent and able to handle anything that came my way. Now I faced
a situation in which I felt neither strong nor happy. I didn't want
to leave my house, and when the phone rang, I jumped as if I had
been electroshocked. I couldn't sleep at night and I stopped laughing. All I wanted was to be left alone.

Mostly, I attributed my despair to life events. What some people
would have found exciting and even wonderful just wasn't right
for me. After almost a decade of work as an author/speaker, I was
weary of hotels, airports and speeches to big crowds. I missed my
family, my bed, my cat and my own cooking.

I thought my situation unique and supposed I was falling apart
in an idiosyncratic way. In one sense, I was. My particular life exhausted and depleted me. But I now realize my experience of a crisis was common. For their own reasons, many people politely fall
apart at some point in their lives. How they regroup and move on
determines what their future will be.

Growth is the only cure for great sorrow or an identity crisis.
Recovery requires the building of a roomier container in which to
hold our experiences. It helps to put our suffering in context and to
see our lives as part of a larger whole. All experience can be re-
demptive if we ask, "What did I learn from this?"

We can make any experience transcendent by viewing it from
a higher level of abstraction. For example, last year our family was
discussing the details of our daughter's upcoming wedding. After a
few minutes of hashing over logistics and potential problems, I
said, "Let's step back a moment and discuss this more holistically.

Our daughter has found a wonderful life partner. John has found Sara. We are gaining a new family member that we all love, and we are celebrating this wedding at our house with friends we have known since before Sara was born. These next few weeks will always be a sparkling memory in the history of our family." Everybody nodded. Then Zeke said, "Mom, when you talk that way, my wife and I joke that you are 'going meta' on us."

Zeke's term "going meta" is a way of describing the process of seeing a situation from a larger perspective. This allows us to help ourselves and others handle increasing complexity and ambiguity. It expands our points of view from what Einstein called "the merely personal" into something richer and more universal. When we do this, life becomes much more meaningful and interesting.

I suspect that most of us feel as if our lives are both pedestrian and momentous. We all experience ourselves as exceptional and ordinary. Within us, we host libraries of narratives and experiences. And yet we are aware that we share a great deal of emotional terrain with everyone we meet.

We humans carry more or less the same template for growth. We are all born into a certain family in a particular time and place. We arrive on the scene with certain gifts and deficits. Family members educate us about our tribe and its rules. We traverse the same developmental stages and share critical life moments—birth, childhood and young adulthood, the commitment to a partner or a community and the deaths of family and friends. We make choices and are swept away by fate. People, place and time shape our lives just as wind shapes the Nebraska Sandhills.

Most of us eventually face crises of confidence, or what Saint John of the Cross described as a "dark night of the soul." Spiritual traditions have many examples of this: Jesus was forsaken in the

Garden of Gethsemane, and Mohammed was unhappy with his life in Mecca and retreated to a cave in the mountains where he experienced his first revelation from God. Mental health professionals call this crisis a breakdown. I used to do that, but now I call it a gift.

Of course, not all people grow from crises. Some refuse to accept the need for redefinition, and orchestrate their own intellectual and emotional shutdown. Those who do grow manage to stay awake to the anguish, confusion and self-doubt. This requires a high tolerance for discomfort, as well as the ability to see the world as it is, not as they wish it to be. Over time, the people who continue to struggle emerge wiser, kinder and more resilient. After they have broken and rebuilt themselves, they feel less breakable.

Living is a complicated process, a journey of discovery that never ceases. As I grow older, the basic facts of life seem increasingly simple. The closer we live to our core, the more we realize that we are like other people. My fear and sorrow are yours, as is my harsh self-judgment. My desire to be good and to feel loved is your desire, too. We all seek peace.

MELTDOWN
(2002)

The success of *Reviving Ophelia* was my portal into a new, glittery world. Because of it, I've been able to work for the last fifteen years as a writer and speaker, and I have had hundreds of experiences I would never have had otherwise. I thank the universe in general and all of the people who helped me in particular.

My story has been a Cinderella story. Almost overnight I went from scrubbing floors and peeling potatoes to dancing in the ballroom with the handsome prince. I was the luckiest girl in the world, but alas, I didn't have the temperament to be a princess. I didn't like dressing up or being the center of attention. I preferred the role of servant to that of the served. I was more content preparing the feast, darning the socks or sitting among the birds in the garden. I never felt I was meant to be Cinderella. As a scullery maid, I knew my place.

As a quiet person who has loved solitude and reading all my life, I am perfectly suited to be a writer. But I am uniquely unsuited to be a professional speaker and frequent traveler. I am a home-body who prefers one-on-one conversation to parties. I have a hard time setting limits with others and feel badly when I let people down. If I think I have disappointed someone, I cannot sleep.

I have never learned to pace myself. I live intensely right up until I hit the wall and crumble. On the road, I would often be exhausted, and yet I would need to keep functioning as a professional. Sometimes I was so tired I could not think clearly or perform my duties properly. When I didn't live up to my expectations for myself, I was filled with guilt and shame.

Below is a small ode to coming home that I wrote after one of my work trips. I think it conveys my stress from the work and travel.

I am coming home from a Pennsylvania airport, with its bossy security guards who do not smile or speak when I say hello, from its creepy shuttle buses that make me feel like I am a cow being hauled to slaughter, from its loud and meaningless noise, its neon lights and overcrowded bathrooms, and from its unpleasant smells of anxious, sweaty people and greasy food.

I am coming home from the all-day workshop, from 350 pairs of eyes staring at me, from books pressed forward by excited people and from overwhelming kindness, curiosity and intensity that I attempt to match but cannot.

I am coming home from trying to help others with their family lives or work when I am exhausted, hungry and sick. I am weary of smiling, when I am fearful that I'll be stranded far from Nebraska while a blizzard closes roads and airports all over the area. I am coming home feeling guilty that I cannot be a better, smarter and more energetic person.

I am moving away from the cavernous convention center, from the energy bars I ate instead of meals, the anxious event planner who overhandled me and wouldn't grant me time to blow my nose. I bid farewell to the well-meaning woman assigned to drive me to the airport, but who, unfortunately, didn't know the route and almost caused me to miss my flight.

As the plane takes off, I lift away from the chain hotel room overlooking the convention center. I wave good-bye to bad coffee, a sluggish toilet for which I had to order a plunger and the late-night noise of a high school soccer team partying next door. I bid farewell to the four a.m. wake-up call.

I arrive to a cold car in the parking garage of Omaha's Eppley Airfield, to my own icy bottle of water, to folk music by Harvey Reid in my CD player and to snowy I-80 and the farms with their starry little lights. As I cross the Platte River, I inhale the darkness and tranquillity. I experience what my grandfather must have felt when he was driving a team of horses home from Flagler, Colorado, during a blizzard. My grandmother would have placed a lantern in the attic window. As he turned off the main road and traveled the last miles to the ranch, he would search for that light.

I arrive home to solitude. I move back into my body one sensory experience at a time. First, it's the familiar sweatpants, next the taste of leftover smoked chicken enchiladas and then the creaking sounds of my house rocking in the wind. I savor the vista of snow-laden pines, the low pearly sky and the icy lake. I sit in my old recliner with a glass of wine and read the newspapers. I am home. I am home. I am home. There is no greater happiness for me and I find myself wishing that death and its aftermath might be this good, might feel this welcoming.

Almost from the beginning of my speaking career, I knew that the lifestyle of a traveling author was not for me. On the road, I was disoriented, literally and figuratively. After a few nights in hotels, I would be unable to remember my room number and would get lost in hotel hallways. I missed my family, my friends, swimming and my own cooking.

In airport terminals I deeply rued my ability to read faces and voices. I could sense people's anger, exhaustion and stress. I noticed the old woman crying on the moving walkway or the refugee confused by the concourse signs. I noticed the airline employee who was frazzled and helpless as she faced a long line of disgruntled passengers. Sometimes I could hold a crying baby while her mother used the restroom, or I could walk a lost person to his gate. However, I couldn't fix everyone. I soaked up all the emotions of the harried people around me.

My lack of self-protective skills caused me problems. Once, on a book tour, I arrived in Boston after midnight. I had trouble falling asleep, and when I finally succeeded, I was awakened by a fire alarm. I had slept only a couple of hours when my escort for the day showed up to take me for interviews. I plowed through my morning interviews, but by afternoon, when I was answering questions for a ninety-minute radio show, I was exhausted. The hosts poured me strong coffee and handed me chocolates to buck me up. Before I finished the interview, my thoughts were evaporating mid-sentence. Too weak to call off the interview, I didn't have the power to protect myself from talking when I was no longer capable of thinking. Feeling shamed, I sat there as the hosts pelted me with questions.

I took my work as a speaker seriously, and for the most part I did a good job. But I felt like a failure. I couldn't live up to my own expectations of how I should behave. I could never be smart enough, energetic enough or kind enough to satisfy my own conscience. In my own personal court of law I tried and convicted myself of failing to meet the needs of others, of being a physical and emotional weakling and of possessing the worst kind of moral turpitude—ingratitude.

I had the wrong psychological makeup for public life. My lifelong roles as the family nurturer, organizer and worrier had allowed me to feel confident and useful, but they also made me feel hypervigilant and responsible for everyone's well-being. As a teacher and therapist, I functioned as an emotional and intellectual cheerleader. Now, ironically, because of the number of people who wanted my help, I was becoming a professional discourager. Turning down requests to help others made me feel guilty and miserable. Since the time I was young, I had lived a life of trying to be good to everybody. Now there were simply too many "everybodies."

Because the topics I write and speak about—families, aging parents, teenagers and community building—were of utmost importance to people, many audience members wanted to talk to me about their most pressing problems. People wanted nurturing and advice, yet the settings were not conducive to this. I couldn't give them what they needed and what I wanted to give them. I never missed the looks of disappointment, the sags of shoulders, or the eyes that stopped shining when I had to beg off.

Often I would be hypoglycemic, exhausted and frazzled, and yet I would be meeting people who hoped I would be charming, intelligent and full of energy. They expected me to be present for them and I seconded their expectation. I tried to act properly, but at times I wasn't capable of that. Sometimes I was hurried and brusque with good-hearted people. Afterward in bed, I would lie

awake and worry that I had offended the dear old man with the
long story about his grandmother, the well-meaning organizers
who wanted me to see their kids' drawings, or the young writer
filled with questions about publishing her poetry. Ten years later,
I am still struggling to forgive myself for my lack of kindness.

Once when I was in Tennessee promoting one of my books on a
book tour, I spoke to a group of women who were excited to host
me for an evening event. Afterward, they wanted to share stories
with me, but I was slurring my speech from exhaustion and eager
to catch a few hours' sleep before an early flight the next morning.
As I rushed off to my hotel room, I could see the disappointment
and even anger in their eyes. A part of me found my behavior unforgivable, even though I knew it was unavoidable.

When I spoke at Harvard, the dean of the College of Education
hosted a fancy dinner for me. I had worked all day and the dinner
began at nine at night. I had a flight early the next morning for
another day of interviews and speeches. After the meal, the dean
suggested I "joust" with the eminent guests about my ideas. In my
current state, I was so horrified by the thought of taking on Harvard faculty in a battle of wits that I blurted out, "No way!" To
this day I feel guilty about that. The host was a wonderful man
who had worked hard to welcome me. He had every right to
expect me to be a stimulating conversationalist. I just wasn't able
to deliver.

I have only two speeds: on and off. Many days were intense beyond my capacity to cope. I would try, try and try to do everything
well, and then I'd switch to off. Unfortunately, at the time my
mind shut down, sometimes I would still be in front of an audience
or talking with people in the autographing line. If I could have relaxed and not tried so hard every minute to be good, I might have

enjoyed myself more and found life on the road less stressful. Perhaps I would have had something left to sustain me.

I'd worked so hard for my success and, at last, my dreams had come true. But my reactions to success confused me. I didn't like to talk about it. I wanted to minimize it and even pretend it wasn't happening. I couldn't fathom what was the matter with me. I chastised myself for wresting failure from the jaws of victory. I was so fortunate. Why wasn't I more fulfilled?

All the writers I knew wanted crowds at their readings and lines of people buying their books. Many people seemed to envy me and think I had a glamorous situation. I would have envied myself if I weren't experiencing my life from the inside.

I knew other people were capable of handling, and even enjoying, my kind of life. I had always seen myself as a person who could cope with anything. But slowly I realized that one person's walk in the park is another person's journey to the dark side. Just at a time when I was pummeled with praise and attention, I became emotionally fragile and my inner spirit turned brittle. I wasn't sure who I was anymore. It was as scary as could be.

At the time all of this was happening, I had been free of depression for many years. My life with Jim in Lincoln, my work and friends, my family relationships and pastimes all kept me happy. As a child, I suffered the repeated absence of both of my parents, which wired me neurologically for depression and anxiety. Although at the time I had no words for my experience, I am certain that I was clinically depressed the year I was six and separated from my mother. I suffered periods of moderate depression in my late teens and twenties, but by the time I had a family of my own and work that I loved, I felt safe from what felt to me like the black cave of despair.

My first depressive episode as an adult gripped me when I was eighteen, after my father's first stroke, while I was a student at the University of Kansas. The week before final exams in December, I could neither sleep nor concentrate on my studies. I went to the infirmary and announced that I was paralyzed by stress. A kind doctor diagnosed me with respiratory flu, even though I had only a mild cold, and he checked me into the infirmary for a two-day rest. I think he sensed that I needed someone to fuss over me and bring me tea. Those two quiet days with chicken soup and kind nurses were restorative to me. When I was discharged, I emerged able to take my exams and travel home for the holidays.

The next bout struck in 1969, when I was twenty-one. I had graduated from college and, after a summer in Mexico, flew on Icelandic Airlines to London. I lived in a small room in a boarding-house and worked selling ice cream in a movie theater. During my time off, I walked the city and spent long days exploring the British Museum. I was lonely, broke and utterly unsure of what to do with my life. I'd fled our divided, raging country, but in the process I had left behind everyone I knew and loved. I had put my own needs first and abandoned my family. It didn't take me long to realize that I didn't possess the courage and steadiness to be a solo traveler. I missed the taste of my mother's vegetable soup and the landscape of home.

The third episode was when I was in my thirties. A high-spirited family friend died slowly and painfully from a brain tumor. The year after his death, I had a difficult time getting up in the mornings and I rarely laughed. I felt as if I were slogging through gray mush. My pain was so intense that I couldn't connect emotionally with less traumatized people. I'd go to a party or out to lunch with friends and stare at them as they talked of gardens, softball games or vacations. Later, I realized that the year Scott died, I hadn't taken one family photo.

My depression during the winter of 2002–2003 felt more intense and all-encompassing than anything I had experienced earlier. Situational factors contributed to the despair. I was gloomy about our post-9/11 world, the war on terror and global warming. In the past I had coped with my worries about the world, but in 2002, the world was more troubled and I was less resilient.

I no longer led a balanced life. When I was home, I tucked myself into my study and worked, and when I was away from home, I was submerged in crowds of strangers. It felt as if a constantly widening chasm had opened between the rest of humanity and myself.

My family was of great comfort to me, but my children were now grown and lived far away. Jim was supportive, but with his own therapy practice, teaching, the bands he played in and my business matters, he also was sprinting through his own days with a to-do list a mile long.

My old friends had always calmed me down and made me laugh, but suddenly I was a less available friend, leading a life very different from theirs. They were remarkably kind and patient with me, but we were all frightened of the changes in our relationships. I no longer had time to simply relax with them. When I saw my friends, I felt I couldn't talk much about what I was experiencing. It sounded too much like bragging or complaining.

I had spent my life developing a web of relationships that fended off my dark loneliness. In Lincoln, where I have lived since 1971, I frequented the same few stores, libraries and cafés. In our private practice, Jim and I worked for decades with the same colleagues. To feel relaxed, I need to move among people who are my friends and family. If I don't know where I fit in a framework of relationships, I don't know who I am.

Usually when I traveled, I befriended whomever I was with. I chatted with waiters, clerks in hotel gift shops, cab drivers and book-tour escorts. But I couldn't always do this. Once, when I worked for ABC in New York City, the network hired a driver for me. As he drove me to the studio, he didn't speak or respond to my hello. When I finished my show around noon, I came out for my ride to the airport. I brought us both sandwiches and bottled water. When I offered him lunch, he tossed his sandwich into a trash bin and said menacingly, "You aren't eating in my car, lady."

Another time, I rode with a cabdriver who wouldn't make eye contact or speak to me. Yet when his cell phone rang, he laughed and talked to his caller. I could have been a sack of grapefruit in the backseat. In these depersonalized interactions, I felt invisible.

I know that I am extraordinarily lucky and that my particular traumas were minor compared with those of cancer victims, soldiers in Afghanistan or abused or hungry children. I am a privileged, well-educated and healthy American, and for all this I am profoundly grateful. In a world of famine, wars, earthquakes and sex slaves, I don't ask for sympathy or expect any. I am not writing this to bemoan my fate, but rather to understand it and, perhaps, to help readers understand theirs as well.

Misery spares no social class or culture. External conditions do not totally determine happiness. To say that all privileged people should feel nothing but joy is to assert that all people in dire circumstances should feel nothing but sorrow. While our lives may be different in many ways, our hearts are much alike. We experience the same ever-changing gamut of emotions. Indeed, it is the human condition to feel hope, fear, joy and sorrow. To deny any-one's right to a complete set of human reactions is to deny our common humanity.

Yet I know that in writing about my life, I walk a tightrope. I don't want in any way to compare my angst to the tragedies of those who are struggling simply to live and eat, but yet I want to share as honestly as I can my own felt experience. I don't mean to complain about what has always been a good life, yet I must ex-plain what has been upsetting to me in order for readers to under-stand my meltdown. It was not the success per se, but the makeup of my personality that made my life difficult.

My reactions to public life were rewiring my brain and increas-ing the levels of stress hormones in my body. My coping resources were inadequate and left me chronically anxious and sad. I rumi-nated on past events and dreaded future ones. In the fast lane, I was on a bumpy, scary ride.

Then I became an accident victim. During a book tour, I expe-rienced chest pains and an irregular heartbeat. When I came home for Easter weekend, I saw my doctor, who told me that anxiety was causing the arrhythmia and that my blood pressure was danger-ously high. These ailments were especially frightening because my father had suffered a stroke at age fifty and my younger brother had a heart attack and a stroke at forty. I told my doctor that many mornings I woke with the taste of metal in my mouth. She said stress was causing chemical changes in my body and that soldiers on the front lines often have this same complaint. She prescribed sufficient antianxiety medication so that I could complete my tour.

Back on the road, even with the medicine, my hard-to-control mind now became unmanageable. It shouted to me, "You are let-ting people down. You are neurotic. You are weak." When I had a few moments of clarity, I would ask myself, "Where is that girl who was eager for new experiences and filled with zest? What happened to the competent, content Mary? Who is this nervous, introverted, scattered woman? Where did I go?"

My last speech of 2002 in a small town in the Northeast was a disaster. It was winter and I didn't want to leave home. I had the flu and felt exhausted from a long speaking season. Jim and I drove to the airport on icy roads. As we waited for our flight, dark clouds blanketed the sky. What I most wanted was to lie on a couch in front of a fire and drink a cup of tea.

Jim and I flew on several commuter planes, each of which experienced some kind of delay or mechanical problem. Then we drove a rental car through drizzle for several hours to a cheap motel in a dismal town. On our way to the evening's event, we stopped for chili at a dark and dirty café. I had been reading Eric Schlosser's *Fast Food Nation*, a book about the quality of food that Americans eat. I believed I could taste fecal matter in my chili.

I realized grimly that either way I was in trouble. Was I literally eating shit? Or was I so psychotically depressed that I thought I was eating shit? Whichever it was, the treatment was the same— go home and stay there.

By the time we arrived at the event, my mood was so black that I was speechless, but I marshaled my forces and functioned for the event. Still, in the question-and-answer session, when a rather dim student asked me, "What was the point of your talk?" I cascaded back into despair.

By next afternoon, when Jim and I touched down in Lincoln, I knew I was in trouble. I didn't want to move, speak or eat. Acting normal, pretending to care, smiling and talking all required too much energy. I yearned for a vacation from the human race.

For a few weeks after that speech, I didn't see anyone but Jim. I drank herbal tea and read. I found *The Power of Now* by Eckhart Tolle especially soothing. I wasn't ready for much of what he said, but his encouragement to live in the moment enabled me to enjoy my cat, my fireplace and the taste of toast and coffee. For the first time in a long time, I experienced my body in a positive way. I noticed when it was relaxed, warm or comfortable. I paid attention to my thoughts and feelings. Mostly I witnessed sad ones—my negativity, anxiety and, most of all, my relentless punishment of myself. I heard so many harsh voices in my head that I could barely breathe or think without critiquing myself. I believed myself to be the one person on earth not entitled to happiness.

As a therapist, I could diagnose myself as depressed, but I couldn't treat myself. I had always operated at the level of superego, with its "shoulds," "musts" and "oughts"; yet, that winter I couldn't order myself to do anything. And while I realized my mode of functioning had become disastrous, I knew of no other way to operate. I wasn't good at comforting myself. Since others thought I was fortunate, I felt I owed it to them to appreciate my life. When I told a friend that I was theoretically happy, he looked shocked and said, "You can't be theoretically happy."

I once knew a woman who lived in an elegant house with windows looking out onto stately trees and an English-style garden. She kept all of her shades drawn and sat in darkness to save her carpets from sun damage. I identified with that woman. I knew that outside my small dark place was a bright, interesting world, but I couldn't draw back the shades, open the windows and breathe the fresh air.

A strong foundation holds better under duress than one with cracks. As an adult with an ordinary life, I had the skills to be happy and productive. However, when my life became more intense, I couldn't manage. In the 1990s, I was trapped in a double bind. As I became a public figure, I grew smaller and emptier inside. My foundation of self eroded. In 2002, my past caught up with me. Fault lines, established in childhood, opened up and I fell in.

Perhaps I should mention that between 1992, when I wrote *Reviving Ophelia*, and the present, I have never stopped working. I continued to behave as I always had. I was productive and competent. Mine was a polite, quiet crisis. I never missed an event or a writing deadline. Almost no one but my immediate family knew anything was wrong. I tell you this because I want you to know that at any given time, we cannot know who among our friends and neighbors is struggling with despair.

That gray winter I felt flawed, flawed, flawed. As I sat staring at the sleet and drizzle of late fall, I replayed all of my mistakes, even the smallest ones: the names of acquaintances I couldn't recall, the stingy tip I had left a waiter at a Thai restaurant, or the inadvertent remark that might have hurt someone's feelings. I recalled my parenting mistakes and the ways I let down my siblings and friends. I berated myself for leaving a coat in an airport ten years earlier or for the time I'd dented our car in a parking garage.

I punished myself with my sins of omission, which are infinite. I recalled times when I didn't make the phone call, attend a funeral, or stop by a suffering friend's house with soup and pie. I had never flossed my teeth properly or exercised as much as I should, not to mention I hadn't read the ancient Greeks or memorized enough Shakespeare. I had always been a worrier, but now I felt addicted to worry. Oh, how I could thwump myself when I was down.

I was entirely alienated from both my inner and outer worlds. All my life, I have found it difficult to admit I am feeling anger, fear or bitterness. Ever anxious that certain feelings would make me an evil person or cost me love, I have locked out unacceptable feelings. That winter I dealt with my "bad" feelings as if I were a hanging judge. I found them guilty and executed them as quickly as I could. However, all that resistance created more intensity and anxiety.

Still, even at my lowest, I was aware that depression is the mind's last-ditch attempt to seek help and that, painful as my state was, it was preventing me from further hurting myself. I felt lucky that I had an early-warning system. I caught myself before I turned into an automaton.

I remembered a day when I saw someone who had lost her ability to save herself. Years earlier in Chicago, I watched a woman enter a bakery and snap her fingers at the staff. She shouted at them to hurry and rudely inquired about the freshness of the baked goods. The waiters scurried around to serve her, and the manager came out to oversee this volatile situation. To this woman, the workers had no humanity. Luckily for them, they could go home to their friends and their families and be free of her. But the woman couldn't walk away from herself. She was moving through her life as a machine, neither connected nor connecting. Her sense of entitlement had left her emotionally bankrupt. Most likely, she could no longer even recognize what she was experiencing. When I looked into her eyes, they seemed dead, utterly devoid of hope.

I thought I was suffering an emotional crisis, but now I see it as a spiritual one. I was living my forty days in the wilderness. I had envisioned a spiritual journey as one that moved up toward the heavens. Now I realize that heading down toward hell was an equally promising path. In fact, the most common way that people move toward spiritual growth may be by first descending into their despair. I didn't realize it at the time, but in the midst of all my misery, I was taking my first steps on a journey toward peacefulness and self-acceptance.

FIRST
LIFETIME

BEDROCK

We are born vulnerable, and all of our lives we stay that way. The great givens—genetics, people, places and events—largely shape our fates. We don't choose our DNA, our families or our first language. We have no say in our nationality, inborn talents or basic temperament. We can work with our givens, but we cannot totally escape them. We carry to our graves the essence of the zygote that was first us.

I am the product of two clans of people. My mother's maternal grandparents were Scottish immigrants. Her paternal grandmother emigrated from Ireland as a bond slave and married the son of the French family for whom she worked. My mother's parents (the Pages) were college-educated Presbyterians who raised hard-working, ambitious children in the 1920s and 1930s in eastern Colorado. From that family I inherited a love of learning and a strong moral sense.

My father's Scotch-Irish ancestors settled with their slaves on the Bray Plantation, at McCracken between Ozark and Sparta,

Missouri, in the 1840s. Two of my grandfather's uncles died fighting for the Confederacy during the Civil War. Most of my father's relatives (the Brays) still live in the Ozarks today. They are fishermen, good cooks and natural-born entertainers. From my father's family, I received a sense of humor, a generous heart, and a tendency toward despair.

Even though I was born after World War Two, I grew up in a world that had changed very little since the 1920s. Almost all of my relatives lived in rural areas in Missouri and the Midwest, and many of them farmed. Until I was in high school, no one had television. Education and entertainment came from other people. No one had locks on their doors. I remember old-timers in the Ozarks who lived in cabins and worked their mules in rocky fields. I helped my father wash his car in a ford across the Finley River. I cooked and fed harvest crews with my aunt Agnes in Colorado. I remember when much of Nebraska and Colorado were unfenced and crisscrossed by tumbleweeds the size of trash cans.

My grandfather Page was a Mason, a Presbyterian and a cattleman. He knew everyone who lived in Kit Carson County, Colorado. I often walked with him to the pool hall, where he bought me a root beer. I watched him play checkers and dominoes. After dinner, to amuse his grandchildren, he recited limericks and taught us cribbage and card tricks.

Both of my grandmothers were the leaders of their families. Grandmother Page had been a teacher who helped establish the public library in Flagler. She called me Bright Eyes. As her eyesight diminished, she asked me to find lost pennies or buttons, thread her needles and read small print. Because of her nickname for me, I felt uniquely gifted, as if I had an especially good set of eyes, the visual equivalent of Rudolph's nose. We considered each other to be perfect human beings.

One time when I was around ten and my family arrived for a visit, I asked her what we would have for supper. She said she had made pork chops. I told her that I loved pork chops and she replied, "Yes, I know. That is why I fixed them." That was an extraordinary event in my life. She was the first person who ever cooked something just for me.

My paternal grandmother, Glessie May Lee, married Mark Bray, and they lived near Sparta, Missouri. He was successful at cattle raising and inventing practical devices. One of his inventions was the ignition switch, which he sold to Henry Ford for the Model T. With some modifications, his device is still used today. He also invented a way to keep boxcars cool so that cattle wouldn't die of heat on their way to market.

Mark and Glessie were rich, happy and crazy for each other. They had three children, my father and his two sisters, before Mark fell apart in 1920. He had lost his livestock to disease and was so devastated by his reversal of fortune that he couldn't sleep or stop worrying. Eventually, he became psychotic and committed himself to the state hospital in Nevada, Missouri, where he lived until he died of old age.

When I knew Grandma Glessie, she dressed in cotton housedresses, clunky black shoes and orthopedic hose for her varicose veins. She wore her black hair in finger waves. She made up words such as the color "shit-mucklety-dun" and "old huldy," a name for her most comfortable old dress. Once when I was in the outhouse and she was in a rush, she shouted, "Sweetie, just pinch it off in the middle and come on out. We're late."

To survive without a husband in the home, Glessie took in ironing. She kept her board up so that she could spray and iron while
she visited with guests. She worked for hours a day in her garden
and she canned everything that she raised or foraged. Glessie sold
Avon products, cleaned houses and cared for older people, including her mother, my crippled, arthritic Granny Lee.

I have a vivid memory of following Grandma Glessie as she
fertilized her corn plants by burying a dead perch beside each one
of them. I was young, but she listened to me as if I were the pope.
She had a way of paying attention that made me feel that I was a
person, not just a child. She asked me questions about myself and
gently teased me in a way that showed me how much she loved
me. Even though I rarely had time alone with Glessie, I felt she
understood my situation. She gave me that resplendent attention
we all need.

Grandma Glessie died when I was eight. She was driving between Beaver City, Nebraska, and Sparta after a visit with our
family, and as she drove through Kansas, she had a heart attack.
She was probably dead when her car crossed the center lane and
killed three people in an oncoming vehicle. I was playing outside
when my father called me in to tell me the news. He sat at the table sobbing, his head in his arms. I had never seen him cry before.
It scared me to know that adults could be that sad. I patted my
dad's arm and sobbed beside him.

After her death, I felt numb for a long while. I have never gotten over it, but I have gotten used to it. For years, I thought about
the tragedy that good people with good intentions could accidentally do great harm. I still think about this.

My mother was intellectual and controlled, my father outgoing and impulsive. I inherited plenty from both of them. I purse my lips the way my mother did when she was concentrating. I share her resolute expression and her way of lowering her head and frowning when she charged into difficult situations. I received my father's thick, curly hair, his soulful eyes and his low forehead. My face, like his, is transparent in its passion and emotionality. He was, and I am, terrible at poker.

My parents loved to work and only complained when they couldn't find projects. After long days at their jobs, they would stay up all night canning beans or mopping floors. My mother worked until she was exhausted, then crashed wherever she was. Many a time she slept through church, nodded off when she sat down to read a magazine, or grew drowsy driving and pulled off the road to nap for a few minutes. My father ping-ponged around in whatever space he occupied. People asked, "Frank, do you ever sit still?" I inherited their ways of operating in overdrive. None of us had any other speed.

Both sides of my family were outside every possible moment. It is as if we were solar-powered. My earliest memory is of lying on a blanket outside in the Ozarks. I recall the dappled sunlight and the sway of branches. To this day, I am in the sun every possible moment, and I become gloomy and anxious in rooms without windows. I would rather live in a tent than a basement apartment. My relationship to sunlight and the natural world is so basic as to strike me as genetic.

Counting both sides of my family, I had five aunts, six uncles and sixteen cousins. Our families visited one another frequently and stayed for weeks at a time. Cousins would come for the whole summer. As a child in Beaver City, I slept in a small bed in the living room. I would doze off listening to grownups in the dining room. They played cards and talked far into the night. I found the laughter and the cadences of conversation deeply comforting.

The Pages told Depression stories. One was about a train car overturning and spilling Georgia peaches into a ditch and onto the road. Everyone from the area showed up with wheelbarrows or wagons and picked up peaches far into the night. People traveled home covered in peach juice and, for a change, deliciously full. Other stories revisited local disasters—a man from Flagler fell into a grain bin and suffocated; a neighbor died of a rattlesnake bite after weeding her bean patch; and once, at the county fair, a performing stunt pilot had a heart attack and crashed his plane into the crowd, decapitating several locals.

One frequently told story was of a small community of Mennonites that lost all of its women and children to a tornado. The men were working in the fields, so the women were alone when they saw the approaching black-green clouds. They rounded up all the children and went to their communal barn. As the men returned at dinner, they stood atop a hill and watched as the barn and their families were lifted and blown away by a long, dark twister. When I was a girl, those heartbroken men still walked the streets of Flagler in their old black clothes.

My mother's youngest sister, Aunt Agnes, was married to a farmer and auctioneer and lived near the old homestead seven miles from Flagler. When we visited them, my uncle Clair would set us kids on the table and auction us off to the highest family bidder. Aunt Agnes could kill, pluck and fry half a dozen chickens for Sunday dinner. She made her own sausage, minced meat for pies and tomato juice. She sewed her clothes and curtains, and could deliver a calf or plow a field. She often had circles of sweat under her plump arms. She wore old clothes and didn't have the time or money to be pretty or feminine. I felt sorry for her. I didn't think she had expected her adult life to be this way.

My mother's oldest sister, Aunt Betty, lived with Uncle Lloyd and their five children on a ranch outside Sandpoint, Idaho. Betty taught school, gardened, and picked huckleberries, raspberries and wild blueberries for pies and jam. Uncle Lloyd hunted elk, butchered them for meat and tanned their skins to make winter coats for his family of seven. One Christmas, he sewed me a fringed, white buckskin jacket.

In spite of his generous gift to me, I was afraid of Lloyd. He was a stern father who whipped his kids and thought children should be quiet around adults. When his daughters came of age, he told them, "Don't get pregnant, but if you do, come and tell me. I'll get my shotgun." I don't believe I ever spoke when he was in the room.

Aunt Margaret and Uncle Fred lived in Whittier, California, in a modern home filled with light, art and flowers. When we visited them in the late 1950s, their lives seemed golden. At the time, citrus groves sparkled around Los Angeles and an orange-lemony fragrance wafted over their neighborhood. Eucalyptus and palm trees lined the streets. Bougainvillea and wisteria flowed over the fences.

What I remember best is the political fund-raiser for a group called Americans for Democratic Action that Margaret and Fred hosted our last night in town. Caterers served cocktails and appetizers, a new and exciting concept to me. I stood by groups of animated, conversing adults as I nibbled on black olives and chunks of Gouda and Brie.

Margaret and Fred socialized with artists, people in the movie business and politicians. Many of their friends at this party were refugees from Europe who had thick accents and numbers tattooed on their wrists. One man was about fifty, very thin, and totally alone in America: He had lost his entire family in the Holocaust. He lived above the small bookstore that he owned and devoted his free time to finding out where and how his family members had been murdered. At ten, I was overwhelmed by this man's circumstances. I couldn't believe a person could survive all that grief and still be alive, sipping wine and talking about California politics. It felt wrong for me to do something as ordinary as eat snacks in the presence of such stored sadness.

Aunt Margaret told me that if I lived my life as a nonreader, I could experience seventy or eighty years of the world, but if I read, I could enjoy three thousand years of the world's most enlightening thoughts and stories. Margaret explained the universe to me as she went along. She was highly opinionated. "You need to read all of Pearl S. Buck, though her later books were inferior to her earlier ones." "You should live in Paris, Rome or New York in your twenties." "Never trust anyone who uses the word 'frankly.'"

Her ideas and examples allowed me to develop a kind of bifocal vision. I had a set of ideas to contrast with those I understood from my life in small-town Nebraska. She taught me that while everyone has a unique point of view about the universe, some people's positions are more informed and interesting than others'. I learned from her that no one's ideas were unassailable. I heard her assail my father's and my uncle's opinions almost daily.

When Aunt Margaret visited, she would ask me to help her pick peas, destone cherries or simply go for a drive. She pushed me to go beyond family training or conventional wisdom and sort things out in a way that fit my own experience. She was gifted at making distinctions and connections. I remember her saying of a man, "He had an interesting life, but he is not an interesting person." About pennypinchers, she quoted Oscar Wilde, "They know the cost of everything and the value of nothing." She cared a great deal that I be exposed to what she thought was beautiful and important.

My father's oldest sister, Grace, lived in the Ozarks all her life. In 1928, when her beau Otis was eighteen and Grace was sixteen, they eloped and married. It was Halloween and Grace wore a beautiful black dress. The young couple tried to live with Otis's family, but Grace couldn't stand their fighting, and they moved into an abandoned chicken coop on the property. As Grace put it, "It was small, but it was our chicken coop."

In the 1950s, my uncle Otis ran a one-room gas station, post office and general store in Bruner, Missouri. As a child, I thought his job was to sit on the front porch talking to people as they filled their cars up with gas or drank their soda pop or ate a candy bar. Aunt Grace raised songbirds to sell and painted watercolors. She was gifted at understanding people. I was on a book tour in Seattle when her son, my sixty-seven-year-old cousin, Otis Jr., died. I called her to see how she was coping. She said, "We'll just have to love and take care of the ones who are left."

My warmhearted, laughing Aunt Henrietta was gifted at hospitality, and her husband, Uncle Max, was a world-class storyteller and charmer. Over the years, Max farmed and ran the Sears, Roebuck store in Ava, Missouri. Once, when a customer called him a liar, Max told her, "If you were a man, I wouldn't let that pass, but since you are a woman, I suggest you quickly walk out of my store and never come back." Henrietta is now my only link to a generation of people I loved. She is the one person left who remembers me when I wore diapers.

Aunt Henrietta and Uncle Max's son, Steve, was five years older than I, and he was just the grandest cousin imaginable. The summer I was ten, he lived with us in Beaver City. Even though he was only in junior high school, Steve organized outings and games and told us stories of his adventures in the wild outdoors. He'd settle disputes, make us laugh and keep us safe. To borrow Thoreau's phrase, he was a "captain of the blueberry pickers."

Every summer we drove from Nebraska to spend two weeks in the Ozarks. Our extended family would set up camp along the Finley River or by Bull Shoals Lake. My father, my uncles and Steve would spend the night in the boat and return with catfish to fry for breakfast. During the day while the men rested, Steve took us children fishing until it grew hot; then we'd go swimming.

My ideas about heaven spring from these Ozark vacations. We were outside twenty-four hours a day, beside clear water with people we loved. We'd catch crawdads and boil them for lunch in a tin can. We'd float down the rivers in inner tubes and dive off rocks and frolic in swimming holes. We'd swim for hours, resting on splintery wooden docks like turtles in the sun. In the evenings, we children would sit around the fire and talk about snakes, leeches and tarantulas.

I often reflect on Steve's kindness. Even though he looked after his brother and four young cousins all day long, he never grew petulant. He didn't have an ounce of bully in him. He was interested in our points of view. He taught me—all of us, really—how people should get along.

My extended family offered me an education in point of view. I puzzled over the different rules for children. Our parents weren't exactly strict, but we children were not allowed to disturb adults.

What we were told to do, we did. Pronto. Still, we had more playing time than my cousins who lived on farms. Aunt Betty's kids
from Idaho had to be in bed at seven at night and couldn't go to
movies, wear shorts or listen to rock and roll. Aunt Margaret let
her twelve-year-old daughter do pretty much anything she wanted,
including wear makeup and date boys.

From my father's family, I inherited the ability to read people's
faces and voices. This is a curse and a burden. It's like having a
good sense of smell—it's nice when you are walking through a
rose garden, not so nice when you are driving by a feedlot. I can
intuit joy, friendliness and peace from people, but also I can read
misery, anger and anxiety. I can tell when people don't like me,
which is not a talent I would wish on anyone.

I was born sensitive and intense. I took everything in. I remember strong feelings about events when I was very young—I wanted
to be good, I couldn't bear to see anyone suffer, and when I was
upset, I was inconsolable. As a child, I cried when I saw boys hurt
grasshoppers or use a magnifying glass to burn ants. When I told
ghost stories to my sister and two brothers, I scared myself into
hours of insomnia.

No one on either side of my family was a good sleeper. As a
three-year-old, I was sent to day care in Denver while my mother
attended medical school. After lunch every day, a teacher placed us
children on little mats and firmly insisted that we take naps. She
dimmed the lights and left the room. I watched as the other kids
fidgeted, then, one after another, nodded off. No doubt, during
this time, the staff ate lunch, then went out for a walk or a smoke.

I couldn't see anything but a dusky room full of sleeping children. I felt revved up from hours of clamor, and I could no more

fall asleep than pilot an airplane. I would shut my eyes and stay still. I would repeat my prayer, "Now I lay me down to sleep . . ." But my prayer went unanswered. In fact, the less I moved, the more my mind hopped up and traveled around Colorado. I'd wander to the Rockies and picnic by a mountain stream. I'd travel back to our cramped little house on an unpaved street or my grandparents' kitchen in eastern Colorado. My stomach would growl. I'd hear a fly buzzing or a siren in the distance. I'd scratch my nose and play with my hair. My socks would itch. I'd need to pee.

One afternoon I couldn't take it any longer. I stood up. For a few moments, I held my breath and didn't move. Amazingly, nothing happened as I roamed around the darkened room. I looked at the sleeping kids' faces and feet, assembled an animal puzzle and played with the school's only Slinky. It was everyone's favorite toy and rarely mine to hold. As I rolled it back and forth, I failed to notice that a teacher had entered the room. She snapped her fingers and whispered my name sharply. I jerked, then hung my head and prepared for my doom.

The teacher took my shoulders and steered me to my mat. "I can't," I said earnestly. As I spoke, there was something new and a bit desperate in my voice. I realized that I meant it. She realized it, too. She looked at me carefully and a little nervously. She hesitated, then picked up a book. "Can you go back if you have a book to look at?" I pondered that question for a moment, then nodded. She held her finger to her mouth, led me to my pallet and handed me a picture book about the animals of Africa. As she left, she patted my shoulder and warned me, "Stay down."

As I slowly turned the pages and enjoyed the elephants, monkeys, crocodiles and pythons, I knew I had learned something momentous. Books could settle me down and keep me out of trouble.

For the rest of my life, I have continued to sedate myself with literature.

For good and ill, I inherited my father's eclecticism and exuberance. I wax enthusiastic about an incisive editorial, a red-tailed hawk in our white pine, a cup of shade-grown coffee or a new pencil. I swoon at the sight of a full moon or a red fox, and when I am happy, I can feel my heart swell.

I changed majors seven times in college, and if I could have afforded it, I would have explored more disciplines. I am always the one at a restaurant who orders the cuttlefish bronzed with molasses and leeks, or the lime- and cinnamon-crusted frogs' legs. My friend Randy says he can always predict what I'll choose from a menu. He finds the weirdest dish and waits for me to order it. My husband once wrote a song for me titled, "It All Looks Good to Me."

This zest for life has its drawbacks. Exuberant people take on too much of everything and then stress out and exhaust ourselves. We can be professional party starters, but we can also wear out our loved ones. After I tasted walnut sourdough bread from our town's new artisan bakery, I effused to Jim, "The baker of this bread will be my next husband." All that enthusiasm can be grating to someone who does not share the same excitement when he eats a piece of bread.

I also inherited a tendency from my father that I'll call "state dependency." I am swept away by ideas, passions or events, and lose perspective. If I am having fun with people, I'll feel like saying, "Let's do this again tomorrow." Or if I am enjoying a sunrise, I'll find it to be the most magnificent sunrise of my life. My daughter, Sara, recently pointed out that every time I make vegetable soup, I say, "This is the best soup I've ever made."

State dependency can make me fickle. I'll dive into experiences and be intensely focused, until I fall under the spell of another set of experiences. One serious drawback with this trait is that when I am miserable, I believe I will always be miserable. If I am lonely, I'll forget that I have plenty of friends and family and won't be lonely tomorrow. I simply do not imagine myself feeling different at another time.

I am the least handy person on earth. After twenty years of owning a VCR or DVD player, I still require written instructions in order to turn it on. I can't change a tire or program a cell phone, and I shy away from any purchase that involves an instruction manual. By the time I manage to open a piece of string cheese for my grandchildren, they have nearly fainted from hunger.

My deficits have limited me, but they have also pushed me to work with my givens. Over the years, I have found a place for my talents, and I have provided my friends and family with a lifetime of amusing stories.

From our ancestors, we inherit our gifts and talents—beauty, athleticism, charm, humor, energy levels and intelligence. These talents can be both gifts and burdens. The finest innate characteristics can be mismanaged. Athletes can become role models or arrogant bullies. Likable extroverts can become great leaders or convincing psychopaths. Good communicators can be skilled therapists or snake-oil salesmen.

Many successful people have worked to transcend their givens. Their drive to achieve stemmed from a need to overcome their disadvantages. They refused to be defined by what they could not control. We all know stories of the shrimpy guy in middle school who lifted weights until he became a college athlete or the shy girl from the wrong side of the tracks who grew up and ran for governor. Many psychologists see this need to move beyond our givens as a primary motivator for all people.

As a therapist, I learned that people change only when they believe change is possible. On the one hand, if we feel our lives are in the hands of fate, we will adopt a passive stance toward ourselves. On the other, if we see ourselves as improvable, we might work toward change with steadiness and ardor. As a practical matter, it is almost never in anyone's best interest to believe that self-improvement is impossible.

Character structure plays a great role in the development of gifts. The most important human qualities may well be perseverance, motivation, steadiness, altruism and the willingness to sacrifice oneself for goals. A man can be born brilliant, but if he spends his life parked on a sofa watching reality TV, he is unlikely to flourish or contribute much to the common good. A child can be born a slave, yet with courage and wisdom, he can lead his people into freedom. We are given a blueprint, but the blueprint isn't the building.

There really is no such thing as a "uniform environment." Every child in the family has a different set of parents. Parents change, as do their life circumstances. Often the older children grow up in a poor family while the youngest grow up in a more prosperous one. Or perhaps Dad drank when the first children were young, but stopped by the time the last one was born. An easy, loving child is likely to experience responsive, available parents. A colicky baby who fusses a great deal finds himself held by a less relaxed and more irritable mother. A boy who worships his dad is likely to elicit equal loyalty from him. Everything shapes everything else.

Grandfather Page told a parable of a man coming to a ranch and inquiring of the old man on the porch, "What are the people like in your area?" The old rancher asked him, "What were they like where you came from?" The man answered that they were mean, sneaky and dishonest rascals. My rancher answered, "That's what they are like here, too." A while later, another man came along with the same question. The old man asked him about the people in his last town. He said, "They were great people, honest, kindhearted and high-spirited. We had wonderful neighbors." The rancher said, "That is what people are like here, too. You'll have great neighbors in this town." This may have been my first lesson in karma.

All of our lives, we must keep appointments we did not make. None of us plan to be gay or straight, brilliant or what psychologists call "dull normal." No one expects to be blind, crippled, obese or homeless. No one schedules football injuries, car wrecks, hurricanes or bankruptcies. No matter who we are and how carefully we plan, we will all experience shocks and surprises. Unless we commit suicide, none of us schedules our date of death in our appointment book.

Yet we can influence our fates. We may not be able to control our parents' divorce or the death of a spouse, but we can choose the way we deal with our grief. People often think of happiness as the result of good luck, but fortunate people can be miserable, and unfortunate ones quite content. Happiness is both a choice and a skill that we can learn, the way we learn to bake bread or play the violin. Because of our attention and intention, it shines down on us. Some of us possess more advantages than others, but in the end, we all create our own inner space. With the right orientation, everything is workable. The great glory of life is in the wiggle room.

MOTHER AND FATHER

Mother

My mother, born Avis Ester Page in 1918, was the third daughter of homesteaders on the high plains of eastern Colorado. Her mother's maiden name was Agnes Blank and her father's was Fred Page. My grandparents met at Peru State Teachers College in 1905. When they married, they combined the names Blank and Page to form their own book of family.

In 1909, my grandfather rode his horse across Nebraska and homesteaded in Kit Carson County, seven miles from the little railroad town of Flagler. Homesteading involved a process called "proving up the land." He had to build a barn and a soddie, a small windowless house made of earth and prairie grass, and he had to live there for a year. After that, my grandmother joined him. They built a wooden ranch house, a smokehouse and a root cellar.

Bethane Ruth was born first; next, Margaret Agnes; and then my mother, Avis Ester. Agnes Ethel was the last daughter. During the Dust Bowl days and the Great Depression, the family tried to raise wheat and corn, but suffered years of crop failures. They milked cows, raised chickens and ran cattle. The girls carried whips for killing rattlesnakes when they rode out to count cattle. The family read books aloud after dinner, and Margaret played the violin. My grandfather wrote and recited poetry. Sundays, after church, they drove their wagon to nearby Crystal Springs for picnics.

My grandmother planted an elm tree in their front yard. During the drought and the Dust Bowl days, she saved the water from her glass at dinner and showered its contents over that little tree. At sunset she made a habit of walking to the mailbox a quarter of a mile away. During the 1930s, the family burned cow chips for fuel and lived off what little they could raise. My grandparents drank "coffee" made from roasted tree bark.

The wind blew all the time. The family could tell by its color where the dust came from. Red dirt was from Oklahoma, yellow and brown were from the south and west, and black was from the north. In the winter, snow slipped through the walls of the attic and drifted over the girls as they slept. Before bed, they heated rocks on the stove and wrapped them in towels to place at their feet. Early mornings, they awoke in the dark to do the milking before the long school bus ride to town.

In that time and place, no one had much money. The sisters wore dresses made of flour sacks. Betty received one pair of shoes a year, then passed her used pair to the next oldest, who passed hers on to her younger sisters. Agnes always inherited shoes that were falling apart. One summer Avis lost her shoes while playing in a sandy creek bed, and she wept for days. The children received an orange and a candy cane for Christmas. An aunt from Amarillo, Texas, sent them new socks and underwear.

Avis graduated valedictorian from her high school in 1935, the worst year of the dust storms. That last year, she was allowed to skip chores after school and play basketball for the high school team. She walked home seven miles in the dark, the cold and the "snusters" (snow-and-dust storms). Avis was captain of a winning debate team. She told all her friends that she wanted to be Chief Justice of the Supreme Court. Many of them wrote in her yearbook that they expected she would succeed with her goal.

Avis received a full scholarship to the University of Colorado in Boulder, where she lived with a professor's family, watching the children and cleaning the house. She majored in chemistry and planned to be a medical researcher. After college graduation, she taught for a year in the Rockies in a school fashioned from a converted boxcar. Her only pay was room and board with the school's families. Every week she moved to a different student's home. If she was lucky, she slept on the couch. Usually she shared a bed with her students. When her school year ended, she moved to Los Angeles to live with her sister Margaret and brother-in-law, Fred, and to attend the University of Southern California, where she studied for her master's degree in biochemistry.

Avis owned two dresses, which she wore on alternate days. Her allowance was a nickel a day. The bus ride cost two cents each way, and she could afford a three-penny candy bar for lunch. The semester she graduated, Pearl Harbor was attacked and she joined the Navy and became a Wave. Because she had a master's degree, she entered as an officer and was assigned to a code-cracking unit in San Francisco.

In some ways, the early war years were the happiest times of my mother's life. She had exciting work and, for the first time in her life, an adequate income. She was lively, pretty and living in San Francisco, which at that time was filled with young men eager to take her out before shipping off to the Pacific front. Boys from her hometown came through on their way to Midway or the Philippines. They escorted her to operas, the theater and fancy restaurants. During this time, Avis was often asked if she was Frank Sinatra's sister. They shared the same build, coloring and bright blue eyes.

One spring morning, sitting at her desk in her crisp officer's uniform, Avis greeted a man who had been sent to shine her shoes. Frank Bray was an enlisted man, just back from the war in the Philippines. With his curly black hair, athlete's body and sleepy Ozark drawl, he captivated her. Within minutes, she was laughing at his jokes and his teasing. Before he left her office, he boldly asked her to go to a movie with him that night.

Officers didn't usually date enlisted men, but my parents never let rules stand in their way. Avis accepted his offer, and soon they were dining in Chinese, Armenian and Italian restaurants and dancing in nightclubs. In wartime, relationships intensified quickly. A few months after they met, Frank proposed. Later, he told Avis that he was ready to marry her on their second date, but he felt he would scare her away if he asked immediately.

They were married in their Navy uniforms in Muir Woods. Afterward, Frank and Avis were assigned to Hawaii, which in spite of the war was a wonderful posting. Both of them were adventurous and absolutely phobic about boredom. They slept only a few hours a night, if at all. After work, Frank would bounce into their apartment and shout out, "I've got a plan."

They'd drive to a new beach to watch the sunset, or invite couples over to play cards. On weekends, they spent afternoons fishing, swimming and snorkeling. Breakfast was fresh pineapple or papaya and Kona coffee. Frank took pinup-style pictures of Avis in shorts and swimsuits, sometimes with leis around her neck. They served in Hawaii until the war ended and then returned to southern Missouri.

My father built them a little house outside of Sparta, Missouri, which is where they lived when I was born. My dad loved being back with his kin in his familiar landscape, but my mother disliked the clannishness and lack of education of many of the hill people. Her biggest peeve was hillbilly music. Years later, she told me that when she sat rocking me and listening to the radio, the announcer would come on after a song and ask, "Can you believe that little Sally never had a lesson in her life?" My mom told me grimly that she never had any trouble believing it. Soon she grew bored with life as a homemaker and agitated for a move.

Avis applied for medical school and was accepted at her alma mater, the University of Colorado. My father decided to reenlist in the service in order to finance my mother's education. This time he signed up for the Army so that our family could live at the base at Fitzsimons Army Hospital in Denver. When I was nine months old, Avis entered her freshman year of medical school. From that time until she was admitted to the hospital for the last months of her life, she never stopped working full-time as a physician.

Shy and socially awkward, Avis was most comfortable in her role as a doctor, taking care of people. Her highest values tended to be doctor's values—respect for the dignity of all human beings and service to others. People who didn't know her well regarded her as formal and cold. She felt a great softness and tenderness toward the world, but she could not easily express this. No matter what she felt inside, except with her patients, her demeanor was rather harsh and imposing. I could read her emotions, but most people couldn't.

In all of my life, I only once saw my mother lose control. We'd driven into Yellowstone National Park, and as she was getting out of the car by our little cabin, she somehow slammed her thumb in the door. As I looked at my mother's crushed thumb that was turning black and spouting blood, I knew I would never forget the scene. To this day, I recall the sunset light, the angle of the car on the dirt drive, the smell of the pines and my mother sobbing and swearing. She asked my father to give her a shot of Demerol and was irritable with him for not moving fast enough. It was the only time I ever heard her criticize my father. She sounded scared and desperate, and it shocked me. Once the Demerol kicked in, she dressed her own wound and apologized to us for her behavior.

Avis had no use for whiners or loafers, and she didn't tolerate neediness in her children or herself. When I complained about a stomachache or sore throat, she would check me out and say, "You are fine. Jump up and get busy." If I asked for a ride to school on a day when the temperature was below zero, she would remind me that she had milked cows on days much colder. On the rare occasions that I asked for special favors or leniency, she would say, "Dream on."

Given her childhood experiences, my mother considered her children lucky because they had food, clothes and a warm house. To her, suffering was getting a leg amputated after a tractor accident or losing a child at birth. Her experiences had taught her that survival required strength and ingenuity. From her point of view, allowing us to be weaklings did us no service. Humor and sto-

icism were appreciated. Talking about emotional or physical pain
was not.

Yet she taught us gentleness. When Avis left for the office, she
would always say to us children, "Be kind to each other." Once,
when I brought home a subscription blank for the summer *Weekly
Reader*, she said, "I want all the kids at your school to have this."
She called my teacher and made arrangements to pay for subscrip-
tions for the children whose parents couldn't afford it. She never
spanked me and rarely spoke harshly to me. Her look of disappointment or frown kept me in line.

For most of my childhood, I was lonely for my mother. She
spent four of the first five years of my life in medical school at
the University of Colorado. Then we were apart for a year while
she completed her internship there. When we reunited, she became the county coroner and the only doctor in the small town of
Dorchester, Nebraska. Her attendance was required at every school
athletic event, the county fair, stock car races and deaths at the rest
home. Once she was called to deal with a boy who had stuck his
tongue on the side of a truck carrying dry ice. No one could figure
out how to free the terrified boy. Somehow she did it with boiling
water and tape.

When I think of her, I think of Sisyphus. When the work was
done, she had time for us, but her work was never done. She conducted all the annual school physicals, made house calls to anyone
in the county who couldn't come to her, and made rounds at local
rest homes and two hospitals, both out of town. Often she would
work all night and come home to change clothes before going to
her office. If we were lucky, she'd be at breakfast for a few minutes. More frequently, I woke in the morning to the sound of her
car driving away.

My mother's absence made me value her more, not less. I knew she was helping people and saving lives. Many nights I lay in the dark waiting for her to come home so I could go down to the kitchen and talk to her while she ate. I would rub her feet while she told me about her day. From age ten on, I worked in her office sterilizing medical equipment and counting pills. This clinic with its nurses and patients, who were our neighbors, my teachers and my friends' families, taught me a great deal about the private lives of others. When I wasn't in school, I rode with my mother on house calls and to hospitals. I sought every conceivable way to be in her presence.

Even as a child I was impressed by her extraordinary competence. She could sew, preserve food, raise fruits and vegetables, brand cattle, repair medical equipment and extricate people from emergency situations. One day my hair caught fire. The elementary school girls were hosting a tea for our mothers. As I arranged silverware beside the lit candles, my long hair swung across a flame and ignited. I didn't even know this had happened. What I was aware of was my mother leaping over tables and slapping my skull. She had beaten out the fire before anyone else had done more than gasp.

Here are the things my mother liked: camping, the family gatherings, *Meet the Press*, Korean food, bamboo furniture, fine china and linens, Jergen's lotion, sunset walks and waterskiing. Her early years of privation left her with the need for a full pantry, and when she died, she had ten gallon-cans of Karo syrup, fifty-pound bags of rice, flour and beans, cases of canned corn and a shelf of unopened coffee cans.

Now and then, before my father's stroke, she and my dad would dine at an expensive restaurant. She would order a martini and ask for one of Frank's cigarettes. But she would invariably choke on both her drink and the cigarette, thus ruining her attempts to be suave. She and my father would laugh and laugh about this.

My mother couldn't tolerate abortion, the death penalty or dangerous activities such as football and motorcycle riding. She didn't like racism, cruelty or what she called "psych cases." She expected people to buck up. I once asked her what she thought of Buddhism, and she dismissed it by saying that she had no use for people who contemplated their navels and sat around saying, "I am the center of the universe."

My mother did not like to be alone. She grew up surrounded by family and she wanted to keep it that way. When I visited her as an adult, she would wear me out talking. After midnight, when I wanted to go to bed, she would insist, "Please stay up just a couple more hours. Let's bake a coffee cake for breakfast or surprise the kids with some cookies." She showed her love by cooking and talking about the world. I taught her to hug and say "I love you." I think she appreciated that.

My mother's life was fairly happy until she was forty-eight. She was practicing medicine in rural Kansas and my father was working as a lab technician. I was eighteen, in my second year of college at the University of Kansas. My brother Jake had joined me in Lawrence, but our sister Toni and brother John were living at home. By then, she and my father had adopted two Korean orphans, who were four and five years old.

In November of that year, at age fifty, my father suffered a debilitating stroke. He woke my mother early in the morning complaining of a terrible headache. Before she could examine him, he was comatose. She called an ambulance that delivered him to the local hospital's ICU. That morning, I rode a bus back from Lawrence. We gathered around Dad's bed and waited for him to regain consciousness. Eventually he did, but he returned as a severely brain-damaged person. He lived for fifteen more years, but he never recovered and died barely able to walk or speak.

When my mother was twelve years younger than I am now, she was left to care for a brain-damaged husband and six children— four teenagers and two newly adopted Korean orphans who spoke almost no English. (My parents had adopted Jane the year I left home and Kim the next year.) Avis worked long hours to keep the family financially afloat. That same year, both of her parents died, and she dealt with these losses alone and without complaint. I, who had been her confidante, was away at the university "discovering myself." When I visited, Avis looked grim, with dark circles under her eyes, but she soldiered on. I cannot imagine how much she must have been suffering.

In 1992, my mother died in a hospital in Kansas. She had been ill with diabetes for over a year. When I visited her and asked about her health, she would always answer that she felt fine, then switch the topic to my family or the past. She liked me to tell vacation stories from my childhood. The month before she died, she hallucinated that she was delivering babies or making spaghetti sauce for a large family gathering—activities she had done hundreds of times. Toward the end, she failed her mental status exams, except when the doctor asked her math questions. She could still solve complicated problems in her head. For many days I sat beside her, but I happened to be away on the day she died. My other siblings were scattered all over the country and weren't with her, either. I deeply regret that she died without one of us nearby.

I often dream that my mother is still alive. At first I feel guilty that I have not been calling her, then I feel elated to know I can talk to her again. In my last dream like this, she was young and pretty, dressed in a pink shirt, eating lunch in a diner with her sisters. When she saw me, she leaped up and ran toward me smiling and shouting, "Come join us. The food is delicious."

I still use some of her Navy language ("shipshape" and "hit the deck") when I talk to my grandkids. I sing them the lullaby she sang to me, and I tell them her stories. I think of her when I am in beautiful places, or when I eat in a good Asian restaurant. I wish she could be alive to enjoy her children, grandchildren and great-grandchildren. She would be proud that I am a published writer, something she died without knowing.

Recently, when I was making a speech in western Nebraska, an old woman came up to tell me she remembered Dr. Bray from her days as a hospital aide. She said my mother was kind to the staff and never snooty the way other doctors were. She told me that my mother had a deep reverence for human life in all its forms—children, comatose people and the old and dying. She said if Dr. Bray really liked an employee at the hospital, she would invite her to come watch her deliver a baby. She would tell her, "This is the most fun a person can have."

Father

I n 1916, Frank Houston Bray was born into a prosperous family in Sparta, Missouri. At that time, his father, Mark, was healthy and making good enough money to buy the first automobile in

Christian County. His mother, Glessie, was warmhearted and fun-loving. However, when Frank was four, his father had his mental breakdown. Mark grew more and more agitated and finally checked himself into the state mental hospital. He was released a few times, but always reentered shortly afterward. He could no longer toler-ate any kind of stress.

After that first breakdown, Frank rarely saw his father. Glessie eventually divorced Mark, but she never stopped loving him. When I was a baby, Dad took me to visit Grandpa Mark. He was polite to my father, but at the end of the visit, he asked him not to come back. He said simply, "I know it is a lot of time and money for you, and I don't really enjoy these visits."

I can barely imagine my father's life as a boy. When Glessie was not married to one of her many husbands, the family became homeless. She and my young aunts worked as live-in servants for more prosperous neighbors and relatives, and Frank mostly lived outdoors or in shacks. He camped along creeks and foraged for food. He told me that, as a boy, he always drank the water that cabbage was boiled in. One time he mistook dishwater for cabbage water and gulped it down. He laughed when he said, "I was hun-gry enough it tasted damned good."

My aunt Henrietta told me that one winter the family lived in an unheated shed in the woods on a relative's farm. Frank would leave every morning with a single-shot .22-caliber rifle. In the late afternoon, Henrietta would stand in the doorway and watch for him to return. If he came back carrying something—a rabbit, a squirrel or a coon, they'd eat. If not, they would go to bed cold and hungry.

Yet to describe Frank's childhood as miserable would be to miss much of the story. His family was jocular, industrious and tight-knit. In high school he lived with his sister Grace and her husband, Otis, in a happy, if crowded, home. He was handsome, popular and a basketball star. After he graduated from high school in 1934, Frank supported his mother and Henrietta by planting white pines in the Mark Twain National Forest for the Civilian Conservation Corps. When my father talked to me about his childhood, he revisited practical jokes, adventures and good times. He adored his mother, and all his life he extolled her cooking and her kindness. Until his stroke, Frank loved to do what he had done as a kid— fish, hunt, camp and forage for food.

When Frank was in high school, he saved a life. At that time, Glessie was married to a prosperous man who lived on a hill above the Finley River. Frank was talking to them on the front porch when he heard shouting from below. He raced down the hill to see a group of people madly gesturing to the water and shouting, "Help. They're drowning." A father and a son had disappeared. Only Frank dove in and searched the area. First, he found the man and brought him to shore alive. Then he went back in for the boy who, by the time Frank found him, was not breathing.

The Ozark paper carried an article about the rescue, and Frank was considered a hero. But he never liked to talk about the incident, which he referred to as the day he failed to save a life. This strange almost mythical story captures some kind of larger truth about my father's life, which was filled with glory and great suffering. All his life, he was fun-loving, charming and desperate.

When the United States entered World War Two, Frank enlisted and was sent to the South Pacific. His whole family accompanied him to the train station in Sparta. Aunt Henri told me, "We cried and cried. No one in our family had ever gone that far from home before."

He worked as a medic in the Philippines and Okinawa, dangerous and heartbreaking places. As he was shipped around the South
Pacific, he was in submarines depth-charged by destroyers. He had
a tonsillectomy on board his troop carrier. The doctors were short
on anesthetics, and he volunteered to have his surgery without any
pain medicine. Later he told us that it hurt, but not as much as he
had expected.

After several years of combat service, Frank was reassigned to a
base in San Francisco, where he met Avis. He was deeply attracted
to her intelligence and beauty. She was classy. They married six
months later.

My father led a peripatetic life. Throughout my childhood, he
changed jobs frequently and often lived away from our family.
When we lived in Dorchester, Nebraska, he attended the university in Lincoln and earned a degree in agriculture. For a while, he
sold seed corn and animal feed. He worked in country hospitals,
and during the years we lived in Beaver City, Nebraska, he worked
and boarded at the tuberculosis sanitarium in Norton, Kansas. He
would usually come home on weekends and holidays, and he was
always available to take us on vacations.

Frank was a big man with small hands and feet, and he moved
gracefully. Think of a slightly thinner Jackie Gleason. Like Ralph
Kramden on *The Honeymooners,* my dad was hot-tempered, enthusiastic and generous. Our friends and family learned never to
admire or ask about anything of his or he would insist they take it.
Over the years, he gave away one of our cars, many of his coats, a
new television and his favorite camera.

Dad shared other characteristics with Ralph Kramden. He al-
ternated between acting the baffled hero and heroic fool. He
worked at relatively low-status jobs and dreamed of making it big.

He constantly stirred things up and made things happen. He could be the life of the party one minute, and the next he could have an angry outburst that sent people scurrying. He had people laughing all the time, when he didn't have them crying.

All his life, Frank replicated his childhood in the kinds of food he cooked and in his manner of providing food. He fried up organ meats—brains, tripe and sweetbreads. He would make a huge pot of hominy and pig's feet, or beans and squirrel meat, and that is what we would eat for days until it was gone. Frank had no concept of breakfast, lunch and dinner, let alone balanced meals. If we drove past a cheap café that advertised twenty hamburgers for a dollar, no matter when we had last eaten, Dad would jump out of the car, buy a bag of burgers and toss them to us children in the backseat. Like piranhas, we gobbled up any food thrown our way.

Dad was always cooking something up, literally and figuratively. When anyone came to our door, including the postman and the milkman, he would yell to them, "What do you want to eat?" He offered adults strong black coffee, or what he considered the perfect drink—tequila and orange juice.

My dad was a plan-hatching organism, who burst through the door ready to go camping, drive into the country for cream and eggs, paint the shed or wash the cars. One night in Beaver City, he announced that a newfangled restaurant had opened fifty miles away in McCook. We piled into our Oldsmobile and traveled to McCook for the magical new food—"pizza."

He bought us go-carts, pogo sticks, archery equipment and chemistry sets. He took up many hobbies—metal detecting, gun collecting, raising tropical fish, photography, rock polishing and coin and stamp collecting. Over the years, he raised cattle, geese, pigs, pigeons, chickens and goats. He taught me how to pickle kimchi and bake sourdough bread from a pinch of starter.

Frank came from a culture that tolerated, and even encouraged, brutal practical jokes. Once, Frank pretended to be a bear along the trail that Uncle Otis walked on after he courted Grace. He growled and rattled bushes before jumping out at him in the dark. That scared Otis so much that he ran into barbed wire, scratched himself and ruined his one good pair of pants. To my total chagrin, Dad would answer our front door with an entire beef tongue sticking out of his mouth.

Like most rural men of that era, he had little sympathy for animals. He couldn't afford sentiment. He raised rabbits, which we children named and played with all summer long. In the fall, he would kill them, hang them up in a tree and skin them. That night he'd serve rabbit for dinner. We were sensitive children, and this experience caused us all to suffer.

Frank was capable of great moral actions and monumental blundering. I've seen him race with my mother toward a burning car to pull out accident victims. I have heard him tell crude jokes and employ racist language. He was the kindest and cruelest of fathers. On our family vacations in the Ozarks, he would spend day after day in the hot sun driving a boat for the water-skiers in the family. Yet, with little provocation, he could explode irrationally at one of my brothers and berate him until relatives had to intervene.

I avoided my dad's anger by working hard to please. My sister Toni was Dad's favorite, and she, like me, escaped the worst of it. He was much harsher with my brothers. I have no doubt he would have sacrificed his life for any of us, yet he lived in the shadow of his father's insanity. He was fearful that his children were cursed,

and desperate that we not make mistakes or act crazy—things normal children do constantly.

Now, as an adult and a therapist, I can hypothesize and explain
his behavior. But as a child I suffered considerably from the effects
of his parenting. When my father drove up to our house, I was
never sure whether to feel happy or nervous. I grew up scanning
the atmosphere for potential trouble and working vigilantly to
head it off. By the time I was in kindergarten, I was extremely at-
tuned to the needs of others and absolutely dismissive of my own.

My one luminous memory of my father is of a night in 1955 we
spent together in Port Isabel, Texas. Every Christmas that we lived
in Beaver City, Dad drove us to the Gulf Coast for a two-week
vacation. The year I was eight, we stayed on Padre Island at the
small Surf Hotel. One night Dad and I went fishing alone on a
wooden dock. As I watched him cast and reel, I savored the warm
air, the crash of the sea and the briny smell of the water. The full
moon rose over the Gulf, and lights sparkled from the little boats
and the village. Dad caught various exotic fish and hummed Glenn
Miller songs. He bought me an orange soda and himself a six-pack
of beer, and he smoked as he watched his lines and told me stories
from his childhood.

I remember being conscious of being conscious. (This was perhaps my first experience of "going meta.") I felt happy, safe and
hyperaware of what I was experiencing. I wanted to remember my
father humming and pulling in fish, my nubby, striped jumper,
white T-shirt and bare feet on the splintery dock. I wanted to forever hold in my heart and mind the silvery moonlight, the tartness
of the orange soda and the staccato red lights of the fishing boats
rocking in the water. Such peace and joy with my father were rare
and significant.

When I was eighteen, my father had his cerebral hemorrhage. After many months of rehabilitation, he recovered slightly, but he never functioned normally again. He lost most of his speech and eyesight and was paralyzed on one side of his body. When he wanted a blanket or a cigarette, he could say only, "Fuck. Fuck it." Or, "God damn it all to hell." He called coffee "aluminum whiskey," which was something we could laugh about.

There is a reason to call what happened to Frank a stroke. Like a stroke of lightning, it came out of nowhere and devastated all of our lives. From my father's stroke, I learned to my core that life could change in seconds. I stopped taking time for granted.

Over the next fifteen years, he would make a little progress with his speech or movement, then have another stroke that wiped it out. For a while, he was able to ride his lawn mower around the small Kansas town where he lived with my mother and siblings. He could carry on simple conversations. He slurred his words and frequently stumbled and fell. Once, when he was around strangers in a bus station on his way to visit me, he was arrested for being drunk.

The last time I spoke to my father was the week of my graduate school comprehensive exams. His words were garbled, but he had called to see how I did on my tests. I reassured him I had passed, but I rushed through the call. I was on my way out the door to pick up pizza for a celebration and I told him I'd call him later. But there was no later. That night he suffered another stroke and lapsed into coma. That time, the doctors didn't try to save him: They simply turned off the machines. He was sixty-five years old.

My father possessed great virtues and terrible flaws, and he dwelt in contradictions. He loved my mother, but he couldn't live with her. He was bright and college-educated, but he talked like a hick. No one tried harder to do the right thing, yet he continually sabotaged himself. For example, when he visited my mother's family, he would often repair or install something. Because of his drinking, swearing and lack of education, my grandparents didn't approve of him, but they would feel grateful for his help with the house. However, just when they might be ready to soften toward him, he would tell a crude story, fart or belch loudly and be back in the doghouse.

Frank suffered a deep sense of shame about both his family of origin and our chaotic family. When Dad met my husband's family, he pulled me into a corner and whispered, "Stay with them. They are a better family than we are." He struggled all his life to find his place in the world and he never did. He died in the saddest way imaginable for an intelligent, restless man: bored, useless and immobile.

EVEN TODAY, I can't totally sort out my feelings toward my father. His life as a parent was sandwiched between a distressed childhood, wars and horrific years as a stroke victim. Maybe if he had remained alive and healthy, he and I could have talked things through and I could have developed a more integrated understanding of him. Because I knew my mother when I was an adult, I can think of her as a person with a life separate from mine. But my memories of my father are encoded from a child's point of view.

Yet even if I had known my father as a healthy adult, I am not sure I would be able to understand him. He was as tangled in generosity and thoughtlessness as anyone I have ever known. My memories of our interactions contradict each other. He could turn my heart to butter and to stone. Across the broad landscape of time, I can't remember who he truly was.

Now I am old enough to understand one of the saddest facts of life—everyone has his reasons for how he behaves. Dad had demons that he never successfully wrestled down, and of course, he hadn't grown up with a father. I suspect he also inherited some tendencies toward mental illness. He never found a comfortable spot in the world. Perhaps if he had lived a long, healthy life, he would have found peace.

My parents' relationship with each other was impossible for me to decipher. What I remember with the eyes of a child was its turbulence, energy and humor. Dad would return home on weekends and yell at my mother for the messy house and out-of-control children. She'd listen without reaction and continue to do as she damn well pleased. Later they'd decide to pick apples and put up a batch of apple butter.

When I was a girl, my parents were not physically or emotionally demonstrative with us or with each other. I never saw them kiss or heard them say "I love you." They showed love by action. Dad kidded my mother and gave her silly nicknames, and she liked that well enough. My mother expressed affection by very carefully administered words of praise. Her heart could be breaking and she would remain matter-of-fact.

As an adult, I have heard such different stories about my parents. Aunt Margaret told me that when they were first married, Frank couldn't keep his hands off Avis and he would ask constantly, "Did you ever meet a more beautiful and intelligent woman?" Aunt Henrietta told me that when Frank and Avis lived in the Ozarks the year I was born, Dad would drink too much and make my mother cry. She said, "Your father didn't always treat your mom right."

When Dad met my mother, he was an Ozark Mountains good old boy, yet he pursued my highly educated mother, encouraged her to go to medical school and followed her as she moved her practice from one small town to another. He was both proud of her and out of his league. My mother respected my father's intellect, energy and skills. She had plenty of fun with him and managed to ignore or gloss over his many flaws. However, she was a driven, independent woman who lived to work. She didn't spend much time worrying about anyone's needs but her patients'.

After Dad's death, my mother idealized her mate, as many bereaved people do. She forgot about his drinking and his temper, and instead revisited the things she loved about him. She said, "He never bored me. He always had a story, a joke or a new idea about what to do for entertainment."

She also said, "I never met anyone except your father who needed as little sleep as I do. We could keep each other company all night long."

THE GLAD GAME
(1947–1965)

Early Years

On October 21, 1947, sixty-eight years to the day after Thomas Edison successfully tested the lightbulb, I was born. I was the first child of Avis and Frank Bray, recent veterans of World War Two, then living near Sparta, Missouri. My father ran a one-room general store, while my mother, with her master's degree in biochemistry from the University of Southern California, stayed home to care for me in a rural area surrounded by whiskey stills, mules and in-laws.

The first nine months of my life, I received a great deal of my parents' attention. My mother told me that when my father walked in the door after work, he would put on Duke Ellington's song "Ebony Rhapsody" and dance me around the living room. She said that for the first time since she was seventeen, she was unemployed and had nothing to do all day but cuddle and talk to me.

Then we moved to Denver, where my mother started medical school and my father reenlisted in the Army. I lost regular contact with my Ozark family and my grandmother Glessie. One month after the move, my brother Jake was born. Soon afterward, my dad was ordered to Korea to serve in the Korean conflict. Jake and I were entrusted to various lackadaisical babysitters while my mother attended classes and studied. Paradise vanished.

In the next four years, my father came home twice on leave. He always returned with gifts from what we then called "The Orient." Once, he presented me with a small thick carpet that depicted a Japanese village and had my name woven into it. I still use that sturdy rug. On one of his visits, my mother became pregnant with my brother John, who was born when Jake was barely out of diapers.

As he left for his last tour of duty, my dad tried to tell me good-bye. He came down the steps dressed in his uniform with a duffel bag slung over his back. I was riding my tricycle in front of our house, and I wouldn't slow down or even acknowledge him. He stopped me, but when he knelt down to kiss me, I turned my head away. He begged me for a good-bye kiss. I looked at him steely-eyed and said, "You'll be sorry you left me, Daddy." My mother told me later, "He was already sorry, and that made him sorrier."

When Dad returned from Korea to our family in Colorado, he and my mother made the fateful decision to split up our already much separated family. I was told that my mother needed to be alone for her last year of medical school so she could concentrate on her studies. Who knows what really happened? I have no memory of saying good-bye to my mother. I suspect I was in shock.

John was sent to live with my mother's parents. Dad moved

with Jake and me to a trailer behind his sister Grace's house in the Ozarks. He must have called our mother from time to time, but I don't remember that. Dad attended college at Southwest Missouri State in Springfield, and at five, I entered first grade in Sparta. Jake, my cousin Karleen and I rode a school bus into town. After school and on weekends, when the weather cooperated, Jake and I played tag or had clod fights outside the trailer. When the weather was inclement, we stayed inside our cold, cramped home. I cleaned the trailer, fixed us little snacks and read to Jake. Otherwise, we lay in our beds and slept or daydreamed.

On nights Dad didn't return in time for supper, Aunt Grace would invite us to her house. Jake and I would sit in the yellow booth in Grace's bright kitchen and gobble down biscuits, red-eye gravy and greens.

That school year I was a sad, distracted girl with little energy for arithmetic or phonics. I remember only one scene from the school in Sparta. I became friends with a quiet boy who also liked to read. Kenny and I sat by each other at lunch and on the school bus riding in from the country. One day we happened to be alone by the piano during recess, and Kenny invited me to sit by him. He played "Flow Gently, Sweet Afton" for me, then put his arm around me and gave me a happy kiss on the cheek. At that moment the teacher walked in and "caught" us. She was infuriated, and after the other students came back from recess, she made us stand in front of the class and confess to kissing. We had to promise not to do any more dirty things. Kenny and I never spoke to each other again.

That year I lost my basic trust in the universe. I fell into a kind of hibernation, as if I'd been put into a closet for storage. My outwardly calm behavior belied an inner emptiness. Thank goodness

I had Jake, who shared my loneliness. I occupied myself comforting him. There is one picture of us from that time. We are standing on the steps of the school in Sparta. We are dressed in ill-fitting coats, looking bereft and bedraggled, and we are holding hands.

In June 1954, my sister was born, and a few weeks later, my mother graduated from medical school. I had known my mother was pregnant and I prayed for a sister. In their usual odd way of empowering me even as they left me with little guidance, my parents told me I could name the new baby. After months of deliberation, I chose Antoinette for a girl's name, with the nickname Toni. This was because of Marie Antoinette, with whom I was obsessed.

The world looked clean and new the morning Dad told Jake and me that we had a new sister. The two of us tumbled out of the dark trailer and ran through the pasture shouting, dancing and hugging each other. The tall grass was soppy with dew; bees and butterflies circled the wildflowers, and the heat of the sun soaked into our bodies. We knew that Toni's birth meant that we could see our mother again. We felt so joyous that we kept falling down into the wet grass and laughing.

In July, my father packed our meager possessions into our Chevy and drove us from the Ozarks to a small town in eastern Kansas. My mother picked up John and Toni in Flagler and drove from Colorado to meet us. At sunset, Dad, Jake and I arrived at the rendezvous point and we waited in our car for our family to appear. At first I was hungry, excited and impatient, but as time passed I grew drowsy. Focusing on the red tip of Dad's cigarette, I fell asleep in the backseat with Jake.

I awoke to my mother's gentle voice. "We're here, Mary," she said. "Would you like to hold your new baby sister?" She smiled and handed me Toni. I cradled the warm bundle to my chest and cooed at her. By the streetlight, I could see her tiny features, her long lashes and silky white hair. I made a fuss over my sister, but really it was my mother I yearned to hold. At least she was nearby talking to Jake and Dad.

Half asleep, I entered one of the happiest moments of my life. My family was reunited. I could hear Toni's breathing and my dad's deep laughter. Jake snuggled beside me, holding Toni's little hand. I could smell the bologna sandwiches my mother was unpacking. In the front seat, I could see John, a much bigger boy than when we had said our good-byes. We were together again. Something that had been dislocated deep inside me shifted back into place.

In my fantasy about the future, my parents would love and enjoy each other and spend lots of time with us children. Mother would sew me dresses and bake us delicious Lady Baltimore cakes. My brothers and sister and I would play together and maybe adopt a puppy. I'd enjoy hours a day with my mother reading to me and telling me stories.

The night of our reunion, we convoyed to Dorchester, a sleepy Nebraska town of three hundred fifty people. We moved into a small house near the old-fashioned red-brick school, and my mother opened her first clinic just off Main Street. My dad enrolled in school at the University of Nebraska, forty miles away in Lincoln. Although he spent most of his time fishing or at the pool hall, he did well in his classes in agriculture. With his natural intelligence and charm, he talked his way through college.

Our parents were mostly absent from the lives of us children, but still, life improved considerably. I knew that my mother was only a few blocks away and that she would come home at night. She had hired a live-in housekeeper, Mrs. Jackson, to watch us.

Mrs. Jackson kept the place neat and baked cinnamon rolls and prepared wonderful meals.

Mrs. Jackson dutifully supervised us older three children, but she loved Toni as if she were her own baby. She was so fiercely protective of her charge that if Toni even whimpered, she would shout, "What did you kids do to her?" We learned to stay far away from Toni when Mrs. Jackson was around. Still, we didn't resent her care of Toni. It was comforting to us. John, Jake and I were accustomed to fending for ourselves.

Mother's practice started slowly; at first no one in town trusted a woman doctor. However, after she repaired the broken leg of a respected farmer, he spread the word around that "Dr. Bray is okay by me. She's as good as a man doctor." Soon she was busy. She delivered babies, made calls at nursing homes, conducted school physicals, dealt with suicides and farm injuries, performed eye and gall bladder surgeries and treated people for cancer and heart problems. Every day, she drove to see her patients in hospitals in the nearby towns of Crete and Friend.

My mother kept her hair short, permed and dyed auburn. Her only makeup was dark red lipstick. At her office, she wore high heels and a business suit under her white coat. At home, she favored housedresses and low sandals that soothed her bruised and swollen feet. When she was around the house, she read me stories or talked to me as she worked. Being near my mother, even though she was busy with her medical practice, I started growing again.

We children cavorted around our old clapboard house and played with one another in our weedy yard. I was crazy about Toni and carried her around like a doll. I decided that when I was a mother, I would have ten children, five boys and five girls, and I would give them names that rhymed.

In the fall, Toni and John stayed home with Mrs. Jackson while Jake and I attended elementary school. Dorchester had a large Czech population, and most of the children spoke only Czech at recess. Baseball and football games, church and holiday programs, and *kolache* feeds were the entertainment. We ate a lot of *jaternice*, liver dumplings, roasted goose and sauerkraut.

One morning the year I was eight, on the playground at school, I was struck with severe stomach pain and nausea. The teacher drove me to my mother's office, where she diagnosed me with an acute appendicitis. She finished with her patients, and then she drove me to the Crete hospital. She scheduled me for an emergency appendectomy the next day with one of her colleagues. After my mother checked me in, she left to make house calls and didn't return until the next day. I lay alone in a white room and recalled all the stories my mother had told about people dying in surgeries. This was in a pre-television era, and of course, I could have no dinner. I had no books or distractions, and my vivid imagination overtook me.

As I lay trembling in the white room in my high white bed, I conceptualized the knife cutting into me. At dusk, when the doctor came to give me a shot to "put me to sleep," I was so frightened that I, the most compliant of children, refused. When he and the nurse tried to wrestle me down for the injection, I bit the doctor. He stormed off, muttering about my wildness. Afterward, I lay in bed, more fearful of my mother's reprimand than of my upcoming operation.

I awoke the next afternoon sore from the surgery and my wrestling match with the doctor. My smiling family surrounded me. Dad held a half-gallon of peach ice cream and a pack of black licorice. My brothers and sister were climbing onto my bed. My

mother had planned her rounds for the time I would most likely
wake up. She rushed into my room in her white coat and stetho-
scope. She said sternly, "We'll talk about your behavior later," but
then she leaned over the bed to examine me. I felt loved. I was
at peace.

My year in third grade was rough. Shortly after my surgery, our
teacher insisted that each of us stand in front of the class alone and
sing all the verses to "The Star-Spangled Banner." I was overwhelmed by the idea. I couldn't sing well and I never spoke in
class. I begged her to let me recite the song at recess, but she refused. Finally, the dreadful day dawned when it was my turn to
sing. I had the song memorized and I planned to recite it.

When she called my name, time stopped. The room began to
spin and my mouth turned cottony dry. I could barely move my
heavy legs through the thick air to the front of the class. When I
stood before my classmates, my mind went blank. I looked across
the room at their eyes, some indifferent, some mocking and others
genuinely kind. For what seemed like forever, I stood motionless
and mute in front of all those eyes. Finally, the teacher grudgingly
ordered me to sit down. Again, I experienced a sense of heaviness
as I walked, as if I were in mud two feet deep. I didn't tell my parents what happened, but for the rest of that year I never recovered.
I had nightmares about going to school, and I never again looked
that teacher in the eyes.

In 1956, when I was nine, we moved to Beaver City, Nebraska.
Dad told us that our mother worked too hard in Dorchester and we
were going to a town where she might be less busy. But Beaver
City was a larger town with no other doctor in the area, and my
mother was immediately swamped. Dad bought land to raise cattle and pigs. Mrs. Jackson moved with us and continued to care for

Toni and our house. But we older three children were mostly on our own. We grew up as uncontrolled as Russian thistles.

My parents expected us somehow to know things without being taught them. When we went to school, we didn't know how to tie our shoes, comb our hair or behave in public. One summer, Dad ordered us to pack our own bags for a trip to the Ozarks. Jake was seven, and all he packed were socks and a toy gun. He was punished harshly for his mistake.

We were not a well-organized family. All six of us were the kind of people who lost our mittens every time we left home. My parents consistently failed to notice school holidays or snow days, and we children often trudged up the long hill to the Beaver City schoolhouse only to find it closed for weather or Thanksgiving vacation.

As a doctor, Avis was a focused diagnostician and problem solver, but as a parent, she was scattered. At home, she ignored what she didn't care to notice. My father acted on impulse and emotion. Both of them had grown up in a generation that didn't worry much about the inner lives of anyone. They couldn't teach us how to comfort ourselves, because they didn't know how to do it themselves. We never heard those things many parents tell children such as "Nobody's perfect," or "Tomorrow is another day." I am not sure my parents believed that tomorrow was another day. They were intense and lived in the moment.

My parents could tolerate frenzy, but not inactivity. My mother once told me she had seen a woman sit at the kitchen table in her own home for ten minutes doing nothing. My astonished mother repeated this amazing fact several times: "Mary, she was doing absolutely nothing."

We learned that when Dad yelled, "Get in the car," we'd better immediately sprint to the car. Otherwise, he was liable to jump in and drive off without us. Once, while we were on vacation in Mexico, he drove away from an outdoor market and left three-year-old Toni behind. A kind woman held her on her lap until my family returned for her.

In Beaver City, we kids would wake up and help ourselves to candy bars and cookies for breakfast. When there was no food in the house, we had the fallback plan of a charge account at the Bridgewater Drugstore. We could purchase Mounds bars or vanilla Cokes, two foods that for many years were the basic staples of our diet. One of my favorite after-school snacks was a bowl of Crisco mixed with sugar.

We were expected to keep out of trouble and not make many demands on our parents. Yet we were high-strung, imaginative and lively children. I suppose we drove them crazy. In fact, I suspect one reason our parents stayed away from home was because we were too much for them to handle. They hadn't socialized us when we were young, and later, perhaps they couldn't. We were feral children, as unruly as a litter of coyote pups.

Wherever our family lived, we were outsiders. In a time when most Nebraskans were eating pot roast and meatloaf, our family ate rattlesnake, *bulgogi* and pickled pig feet. One of my girlfriends said that she never had dinner with us without tasting something she had never heard of before.

Food was just one way we were different. My mother's profession, my dad's recklessness and frequent absences, and both their laissez-faire parenting styles kept us the talk of every town we lived in.

Except for school, our lives were unscheduled. In the winter, we kids played Scrabble and Monopoly. I read books and played jacks and an old-fashioned game called tiddlywinks. My brothers shot marbles and read comic books. On summer days, we swam all afternoon at the town's pool. My blond hair had a greenish tinge from June through August, and I smelled of chlorine. We rode our bikes to the Dairy Sweet or out to Beaver Creek, where we swung on a rope out over the muddy water.

As children we were not shielded from suffering. Our parents stopped to help at every car wreck or farm accident. My mother always carried her black doctor's bag with her. When we came upon an accident, our folks would tell us kids to stay put, then jump out and run to the scene. Once, when we were driving through eastern Colorado, we saw a small plane crash. Dad pulled over, and he and my mother ran toward the burning plane. The people inside were beyond help. I remember being frightened that the plane would explode and kill my parents.

I learned early in life the benefits of being useful. I helped in the garden and the kitchen, folded diapers and swept the floors. My mother, my grandmothers and my aunts all called me a good little helper. When I heard myself described this way, I worked even harder. As a big sister, my specialties included settling disputes, applying bandages and finding shoes. When I was useful, I was loved.

Because my parents had the organizational skills of tornadoes, I was the authority, organizer and comforter. In our messy, chaotic environment, only my room had clothes that were properly folded and books neatly stacked. I tried to fill in the gaps my parents left in the lives of my siblings, but I was a child myself. I felt responsible for much more than I could possibly handle. I grew up hyper-aware of the needs of others and inclined to quash awareness of my own.

By the time I was eight or nine, my parents talked to me as if I were an adult. They turned to me for common sense and empathy. Both of them would preface remarks to me with "I've never told this to anyone but you," then share some story from their past or an observation about their lives. My mother once told me that she had wanted to be editor of her yearbook, but that the teacher told her a boy should be given the most important job. My mother was livid that she had done all the work and Lester received all the glory. And my father showed me the burn scars on the bottoms of his feet that he received when he accidentally ran barefoot over coals left burning after his mother made soap. Their confidences made me feel close to them.

I found great solace in animals. After dinner, our family often would drive outside of town and sit on the hood of our car to watch the prairie dogs cavort in their football-field-sized village. On my parents' days off, we would picnic by rivers or lakes, and we children would look for snakes, polliwogs and turtles. As we drove the little highways to Colorado and the Ozarks, we noted every bird of prey, fox or deer.

My mother told us animal stories she heard from patients. One of my favorites was about a drunk bar owner and his pet rattlesnake. He swore Sugar wouldn't bite him, and he often played with her late at night for his customers' entertainment. One night, Sugar did rattle and nip him, but he insisted she wouldn't inject poison in him. He closed up the bar and went to bed, only to wake hours later with an arm the size of a watermelon. He called my mother and she sat by his side administering antivenom all night long. He kept tearfully insisting, "Dr. Bray, I swear Sugar didn't mean to hurt me."

Over the years our family owned cats, dogs and tropical fish.

My brothers bought chameleons at the state fair, and I kept two blue parakeets named Ernie and Eve by my bed until they froze one harsh winter day in our poorly insulated house. We picked up turtles beside highways and brought them home to play with. At my mother's suggestion, we gave them Greek names—Hector, Achilles, Paris or Helen.

I rescued baby birds, squirrels and field mice and raised them as best I could. We bought coyotes every spring from a neighbor who hunted them for bounty. We kept them for pets until fall when we carried them to the creek and released them, each with a pound of hamburger by his side.

Our dog Pixie came into my life when I was nine. Our family was driving north after one of our Christmas trips to Mexico. We were packed into an Oldsmobile—six people and luggage, plus our usual spoils of bullwhips, painted clay bowls, straw sombreros and duty-free rum and tequila. On the way, my dad had the impulsive idea to buy a Chihuahua.

When we hit the outskirts of Dallas, Dad stopped at a gas station, bought a newspaper, circled classified ads and stood in a phone booth, smoking cigarettes and making calls. His face lit up with the news that a Chihuahua was available. We drove through a seedy section of town to a small house on an unpaved street. An older woman answered the door and let us into a room that reeked of animal urine. Yapping dogs covered every square inch of floor and furniture. Undeterred, Dad bargained. She said she loved every dog dearly but was desperate enough for money that she would sell one—a tan and black adolescent named Pixie Rosarita. Dad paid her twenty-five dollars, and we piled back into the Oldsmobile. We children patted Pixie all the way across Oklahoma and Kansas.

One time, my brothers and I were playing in the backyard when Pixie swallowed a fishhook on a pole left in the yard. She bled from her mouth, yelped in pain and pulled away from the fishing pole, which of course embedded the hook even more. My brothers were shouting. I frantically tried to free her, but she was too crazed to settle down.

After brief but careful consideration, I did an almost unimaginable thing: I called my mother at work. We had been taught we could call only in case of an emergency, which was carefully defined as the house burning down or one of us being seriously injured. I knew my mother wouldn't interrupt work for a dog, but I was panicky enough to be duplicitous. When she came to the phone, I shouted into the phone, "Come home quick, one of us is badly hurt." Then I quickly hung up as she was asking, "Who? What happened?"

She roared into the driveway in a matter of minutes, and in her business suit, white coat and high heels, she caught Pixie and efficiently extricated the fishhook. She didn't bother with any treatment and said only, "Mouths heal fast." She said to me harshly, "I don't like it that you were sly and sneaky." Afterward, I couldn't quite decide how to feel. I had saved Pixie but disappointed my mother. I really did want to be a good girl, but I realized that it wasn't that easy.

During the summers, I built and managed a little mud and sand business that I christened the Bluebird Bakery. Each morning, my mother would order a long list of the baked goods for the end of the day. Out by the alley and the rabbit shed, I had my bakery with its cans of sand, gravel, rocks and twigs, as well as several kinds of mud and pitchers of water. I assembled a row of old boards to hold the bowls and baking pans. The oven was wherever the sunlight was landing. All day I labored to produce chocolate chip cookies, banana bread, pies and muffins. When Mom came home at night, she would walk out to my bakery and I would proudly present my day's creations.

I grew up in a fantasy world of my own invention. Margaret Mitchell described children like me as "hearing the music of the moon." For example, I was romantic to the point of ridiculousness about what life was like in big cities. At night as I listened to trains rattling past town, I pictured the elegant, handsome people dressed in expensive store-bought clothes who were dining in the club car. I imagined the glamorous places they were going—Chicago, San Francisco, Boston, Philadelphia and New York City—places I could barely visualize. Denver and Lincoln were the only cities I'd seen, both of which were pretty sleepy. I tried to envision skyscrapers— such an evocative word. I imagined restaurants with waiters in white coats serving pheasant under glass and what sounded like the most marvelous dessert imaginable: Baked Alaska.

Caught up in my own internal dramas, I missed a great deal of what was actually happening. Consequently, my formulations about the world were often naïve. When I was eight, I saw an ad in a magazine for a puppy in a teacup. I fell for this tiny dog and sent off a dollar and my order form. I walked to our mailbox every afternoon and waited for my puppy in a teacup. Of course, months passed and the dog never arrived. The puppy company was clearly a scam, but I was extremely slow to give up hope. For months, I expected that "Caramel" would show up.

My vivid imagination kept me happily occupied in a slow time and place, but it also caused me great pain. Sometimes, especially when I was worried about my siblings or I hadn't had much time with my parents, my mind's anxious thoughts would come so quickly that I felt out of control.

Reading focused my racing mind. My grandmother Page subscribed to *Reader's Digest*, which was my first authoritative source of information about the world. I remember lying on the couch at my grandparents' house reading old issues about the kidnapping of the Lindbergh baby, the murder of the tsar and his family, and the disappearance of Amelia Earhart. To this day, I recall the details of those articles and I've retained a lifelong interest in these stories. At my grandmother's house, I also read biographies of Helen Keller, Dr. Tom Dooley and Albert Schweitzer.

I deeply identified with girls who coped with difficult circumstances. My favorite heroine was Francie from *A Tree Grows in Brooklyn*. She was a poor Irish immigrant with an alcoholic father. Like me, she was a watcher and a reader, who tried to be a good daughter and sister, and who was filled with yearning to learn. Francie compared herself to a weed tree, growing strong out of the cracks in a sidewalk.

From *Pollyanna*, I learned to play the "glad game." When Pollyanna received crutches instead of a doll in the church charity basket, her minister father encouraged her to be glad she didn't need the crutches. They invented a game to remind them to be grateful at all times. I imitated the "glad game." When my parents didn't come to a school play, I was grateful that at least my parents were alive and I would see them again. This coping device became deeply ingrained in me. As a child, reading along Beaver Creek, I found a sturdy pair of rose-colored glasses, which I wore until they broke in 2002.

My mother encouraged me to check books out of the library

and read as much as I wanted. She had no ambivalence about edu-cated women. Dad's attitudes were more confusing. He was from a place and time that was deeply distrustful of intellectuals, espe-cially intellectual women. He wanted me to earn a good living, but he didn't support my dreaminess and creative pursuits.

He wanted me to make good grades, but he neither understood nor approved of most of my reading. Once, when I told him I loved the smell of books, he said, "Don't tell anyone that, or they'll think you are a pervert." I didn't even know what a pervert was. I also told my father I wanted to be a writer when I grew up. He scoffed at the idea and said, "You can't make a living that way. Be a doctor like your mother."

When I was in fifth grade, I wrote my first poem, a sonnet, comparing life to the seasons. My teacher gave me a big red C and scrawled "Trite" across the top of my poem. I gave up on my ca-reer as a writer. Between my dad's warning and the fact that I couldn't do better than a C in creative writing in Beaver City, Ne-braska, I despaired. I thought writers were born geniuses and that I was a pedestrian person who worked hard but had no real gifts.

Although I was an indifferent student in elementary school, I cherished the routines and the order of bells ringing, sharpened pencils and brand-new paper. I liked geography, especially assign-ments to fill in maps of the United States with states and capitals or maps of the world with their country names, their colonial col-ors, their major cities, mountain ranges, rivers and their most im-portant products. I enjoyed memorizing information such as the word and symbol for tungsten, a product of Peru. I was taken by names like Orinoco and Mozambique. I savored story hour, when teachers read to us.

Yet academic work generally bored me. One teacher wouldn't

let us turn the pages of our books until every child had finished the page and we could all turn together. My brain shorted out at that slowness. When teachers explained school rules or how to fill out a worksheet, I would drift off into a fantasy about my Roman villa or the palominos I would someday own. When I was called on, I often had no clue about what was happening.

From the beginning, I couldn't master the social piece of elementary school. I was a year younger than my classmates and far behind in my physical and social development. Yet I was older in my responsibilities and intellectual interests. The hardest part of school for me was recess. I couldn't figure out how to talk to other kids. I couldn't run fast, catch a ball, skip, or jump rope. Usually during recess I read under a tree.

In junior high, Mr. Swift taught us social studies. He spoke ungrammatically and paid attention only to the athletes. I didn't like him because, among other reasons, he had named his son Steve so he would have the same initials as Hitler's SS. Mr. Swift ran the local pool in the summer and was our swimming teacher. I took all the swim lessons I could, and soon I was ready to become a junior lifeguard. But to achieve this rank, I had to rescue Mr. Swift. He was a tall, burly man, very pugnacious, and not the least sensitive to gender issues.

From the side of the pool, I watched as other students tried to rescue him while he kicked and flailed with all his might in the deep end. All the boys and two strong girls succeeded. While I had earlier practiced and successfully saved my petite and polite girl-friends, I was terrified of Mr. Swift. I was as strong as other kids but not as able to handle the emotional strain of wrestling with him.

I could not even imagine actually subduing the coach, getting a good grip on him and pulling him to the pool's edge while he was twisting and grabbing at me. When Mr. Swift called my name, my whole body clenched into one long, hard knot. I felt light-headed and had trouble focusing as Mr. Swift jumped in, splashed and screamed for help. I thought grimly, "I am the one who needs to be rescued."

Somehow I willed myself to dive in and swim toward what looked like a ten-foot-tall, four-hundred-pound muscleman. He was a good actor as he kicked and yelled at me. When I cautiously reached for his arms, he grabbed my long hair and pulled me under. I realized I could no more save the coach than I could wrestle an alligator or fly from a trapeze. I came up choking and headed for the ladder as if my life depended on it. My goal to be a lifeguard died that day.

In fairness to Coach Swift, he wasn't educated about gender matters, and his task was to teach adolescents how to save drowning people. He had no guarantee that all my rescues would be timid girls smaller than myself. If I had been a lifeguard, my first person in distress might have been a man bigger than Coach Swift. Still, he certainly scared the bejesus out of me.

For every Mr. Swift in my life, I have found a Mrs. Van Cleave. When I was suffering through junior high, my mother asked her to teach me china painting and pottery. I had no gifts in art, but in that time and place, there were few children's lessons of any kind. After school, I would walk to Mrs. Van Cleave's house to learn how to glaze china and to throw pots on a wheel.

I never was much of a potter, but that wasn't the point. These sessions were about salvation. I'd arrive shell-shocked from a place where boys told dirty jokes and tried to look down my blouse and where girls talked about kissing and makeup. Mrs. Van Cleave would be waiting with chamomile tea and lemon bars.

She was a Dutch immigrant, very old and soft, with white braids piled on top of her head. She wore long rayon dresses, thick sweaters and clunky high-topped shoes. She would escort me through her orderly, fragrant house to the pottery room, a converted greenhouse filled with southern light, and we would set to work. With my uncombed hair, dirty fingernails and ill-fitting clothes, we must have looked quite the pair.

Side by side we created our treasures. She would help me toss or coil a pot or apply undercoating to something we'd glazed. She showed me how to paint leaves, flowers and berries. When I left her to head home, I felt safer and more hopeful. Mrs. Van Cleave gave me the gift of two good hours every day. I wonder if she had any idea how much she did for me. Do any of us really know much about the long-term effects of our actions?

About a decade ago, some of Mrs. Van Cleave's relatives attended one of my speeches. They brought me a picture that she had painted of me. In it, I have long golden hair, sparkly blue eyes, a shy smile and a transcendent glow. Looking at my portrait, I realized that, while I felt unkempt, awkward and ugly, Mrs. Van Cleave thought I was beautiful.

When my mother died, I cleaned out her apartment and packed up the pottery I had made at Mrs. Van Cleave's. All those intervening years, my mother had displayed my Christmas angels with their spotty mother-of-pearl glaze and smeared gold gilding, my fat teapot adorned with its purple grapes and golden leaves, and my misshapen mud-colored coil vases. When I realized how long my mother had treasured my pottery, I thought that we never know how much people love us until we are old ourselves. Then the evidence unfurls against the backdrop of time.

All the way through school, my main emotions were boredom

and anxiety. I remember days spent counting ceiling tiles in my classroom, watching the clock stand still or looking yearningly out the windows. In both students and teachers, I observed rudeness, pettiness and stupidity, but most of the teachers were kind to me and, except for a few students, I was well treated and even liked. Yet no one, except my closest friends, ever recognized I had any gifts. I remember one teacher who asked our class, rhetorically it turns out, if anyone had read *Uncle Tom's Cabin*. When I raised my hand, she said she didn't believe me. No one, including most people in my family, had a clue what I was about.

Looking back, I wish I could have just skipped elementary school and junior high. Outside school, I loved talking to people and learning from them. I would spend time visiting with old people in their gardens and on their porches. I liked to play with little kids and chat with patients who came to my mother's office. Almost every day, I learned things about the natural world and animals, and I read more books on weekends and during the summer than I could possibly read at school. I believe I would have learned more if I had just been left alone to educate myself.

Growing up in Beaver City, I had an excellent education on the foibles and virtues of the human race. I observed how kind and how cruel people could be. I studied the various ways children and adults deal with adversity. I observed that good fortune and prestige have little relationship to gifts and virtues. In short, I was educated to be a true democrat.

It is a mistake to think of small-town life as simple. A village of five hundred people contains as many interesting characters and as much tragedy and comedy as all of Shakespeare's plays. Everywhere I wandered, I heard conversations. Women would discuss marital strife or discipline problems with their children. Adults

debated religion and politics, and carefully parsed the moral behavior and manners of those around them. Men complained about
dishonest cattle traders or the railroads. Everyone was an expert on
everything, or so it seemed to me.

Linda, an eighth-grade girl from a troubled, motherless family,
lived with us for a while. After school, she jumped into cars full of
boys and let herself be driven to the country. Other girls judged
her, but I understood that she wanted to pretend for a few hours
that she was popular and desirable.

Lola, an eighth-grade girl from my church, was "seduced" (today we call it sexually assaulted) and impregnated by her father's
hired man. She dropped out of school and church. Even though she
lived only three miles from town, I never saw her again.

Our forever-working neighbor Laura, who had only limited
formal education, had learned a great deal in the School of Hard
Knocks. Her first husband died, and she married a man who was a
widower. Cliff worked at the power plant and was taciturn and
phlegmatic. Laura managed their blended family of teenagers—
Cliff's two large, equally phlegmatic children and Laura's two
feisty, mouthy ones. Mom and I would go to pick up the ironing
she'd done for us, and stay as long as we could listening to Laura's
stories. In an old housedress and slippers, Laura would iron, chain-
smoke and sip on industrial-strength coffee as she regaled us with
Erma Bombeck–style tales of her goofy husband and her trouble-
some children. To this day, I've never met anyone funnier or more
observant than Laura.

The grocer's son, Howard, was badly deformed with hydro-
cephaly. When he was in eighth grade, he tried to kiss another
boy. After that, his life in our town was hellish. No one would
speak to him, and many boys, mercifully not my brothers, chased

him, made kissy faces and called him cruel names. He dropped out of school and simply disappeared.

We lived two houses north of the Snelling twins, whose father was in the state penitentiary for murder. Jerry and Terry were not bright, but they were kind. They never complained about their situation, but simply played with us and made the best of things.

One girl in my class lived with her father, who was dying of emphysema. He spent his days resting in a bed in the front room with an oxygen tube in his nose. Mimi was a brave, responsible girl who cared for her father. Sometimes she invited me to her house after school. Mimi and her father would have a good talk about her day, and then she would serve the three of us bowls of chocolate ice cream.

My mom referred to the family that ran the junkyard as "religious nuts." They wouldn't let their four boys have any medical care, including school checkups or vaccinations. They enforced some kind of weird diet that involved eating only foods found in the Holy Land. The boys couldn't have treats at school or eat in the cafeteria. They couldn't swim or wear shorts, which meant no basketball. Also, they couldn't go to movies or dances or listen to music. Those boys grew up to be wild and angry. Two of them died in separate car accidents. As my mom put it bitterly, "Apparently the one thing their religion doesn't forbid is suicidal driving."

I grew up in a world filled with religion. The Pages were Presbyterians, and most of my Ozark relatives were members of the Church of Christ. When I was young, I accompanied my grandmother Glessie to baptisms in the James River and revival meetings in little towns around Sparta. I would stand beside her, amazed and a little frightened as audience members became possessed by the spirit and shook until they fell down.

My siblings and I were raised in the Methodist Church. Every Sunday, Dad would drop us off and drive away waving sympathetically. Mother would attend when she could, but she always fell asleep during the sermons. As a girl, I conceived of God as male, stern, perfect, powerful and white. I could picture Jesus easily because of all the illustrated stories about him, but I couldn't fathom the Holy Ghost. I read the Bible and prayed daily. I woke early on Easter Sundays to attend sunrise services, and I loved December with its poinsettias and Christmas carols. The Nativity story had great meaning to me.

The Methodists instilled in me a moral code for behavior that holds to this day. Well, not all of it. In junior high I pledged at Methodist Youth Fellowship that I would never drink, smoke or have premarital sex. Those vows lasted until college.

One of my Sunday-school teachers was a fervent young visionary. Lou Anne exhorted our class that if we prayed and learned Bible verses, God would speak to us personally. Under Lou Anne's tutelage, I memorized much of Matthew, Mark and Luke, and many of my favorite psalms.

Lou Anne claimed God had appeared before her many times and that she had witnessed many miracles. Once her naughty cousin Roger tossed her kitten from a third-story window. While the kitten careened to the grass below, Lou Anne prayed for his safety. Sure enough, the cat landed without a scratch. Another time, the Lord intervened as she baked butterscotch chip cookies for Methodist Youth Fellowship. She confessed dramatically, "I forgot to add the baking soda and you know what that does to cookies." We all nodded somberly. As her cookies baked, she pleaded with God to help them turn out okay. And amazingly, "without soda," they did. Lou Anne whispered, "God's spirit made those cookies rise."

Lou Anne primed me for what may have been a miracle by suggesting that God would appear if I prayed with sincerity. That night at bedtime, I dressed in my yellow baby-doll pajamas and tuned the radio to rock-and-roll station KOMA. I listened to Roy Orbison and Elvis for an hour, then read my white leather Bible with its gold-leaf edging, whisper-thin pages and red lettering of Jesus' words. Then I knelt on the hardwood floor, shut my eyes and prayed earnestly. After about an hour, I looked toward our apricot tree and the dark sky beyond. I implored God to send me a sign if he had heard my prayers.

Three times I closed my eyes and beseeched him. The third time I opened my eyes, white light flooded the room. A silver light haloed our apricot tree and the shed by the alley. Just as people did in Bible stories, I trembled with happiness and fear. I kept my eyes on the glimmering clouds and awaited the face of God. At that moment, a full moon broke through the cloud cover. I gasped; then I sighed. Either the face of God strongly resembled the moon or I was kidding myself.

Shortly after that, my faith was sorely tested. The summer I was twelve, I attended an interdenominational church camp in the woods along the Republican River. At this camp, I wandered around the woods alone, praying myself into a few small epiphanies. At sunset, I sat on the wet grass listening to handsome Bobby Umphenower sing "How Great Thou Art." My heart swelled with either religious fervor or lust. I was constantly confusing those two.

I was spellbound by the lectures of the presiding pastor from Oklahoma, Reverend Kindle. He was in his late twenties, but he already looked aged and severe. His belly overspilled his carefully ironed suit pants, and his few remaining wisps of hair were pulled across his shiny skull. His laughter was forced, and when he smiled, his eyes didn't sparkle. The Reverend Kindle was obsessed with sinning. He admonished us not to have sexual feelings when we looked at the genital areas of our friends, something I honestly believe I had never thought of doing until he brought it up.

He warned us that it was sinful to think of human counterparts when someone asked us to pass them a chicken breast or thigh. I had never considered this idea either, but afterward I had odd thoughts when I ate chicken. I would only ask for dark meat or a drumstick, and if anyone else asked for thighs or breasts, I would blush profusely.

The Reverend Kindle cautioned us about masturbation, a word I had not yet heard and didn't understand. His most frequent admonishment was, "Don't think about Jesus when you have a bowel movement." Actually I was surprised he brought this up because one of the few rules of etiquette I had been taught was not to talk about poop in public. After his bowel movement lecture, I thought for a long time about pooping and what was okay and not okay to think about during the experience. Yikes.

I was baffled by that camp and began to question the wisdom of adults and God. When I read *The Diary of Anne Frank*, I experienced a genuine crisis of faith. I asked, "If God were perfect, why didn't he avert the massacre of innocents?" In fact, why did he let any babies die? And what about people who had never heard of our God? Did they go to hell? And why would a perfect, all-loving God punish people eternally for not believing in him? Even I wasn't that petty.

Coupled with my own questions were ideas stimulated by reading Bertrand Russell's "Why I Am Not a Christian" and Mark Twain's "Captain Stormfield's Visit to Heaven." Twain's irreverent ideas, such as "Heaven for climate, hell for company," had a profound effect on my thinking.

Still, I think my faith might have held if anyone would have guided me through my spiritual crisis. Instead, in our little church, the minister took a narrow and punitive view toward doubters. When I was fifteen, I scheduled a meeting with him and voiced my concerns. He said, "You'll go to hell for thinking that way." I wasn't self-aware or sophisticated, but even at that age, I knew I didn't want to belong to a church that didn't permit an open mind. I could believe in a God that appeared to me as a full moon, but I could never believe in a God who discouraged questions.

High School

Dressed in a brand-new plaid pleated skirt and red sweater, I started high school in Concordia, Kansas. We'd moved during the summer so that my mother could join a clinic and, for the first time in her career, not be on call all the time. Dad had supervised the building of our house near the hospital. I was excited about a fresh start, and right away I joined the Spanish Club and Kayettes, a service organization.

I drank in the lessons of Miss Fletcher, a brilliant older woman who in another era would have run a university. She subscribed to *The New York Times* and traveled to the East Coast every year to attend plays and classical music concerts. She recited Romantic poetry and Greek plays from memory, and appeared to have read every book of quality ever written. Even though I made excellent grades and test scores, read her leftover newspapers and wept after reading sonnets, Miss Fletcher overlooked me for the promising male students. This was what all my teachers did in the early 1960s. I accepted it and felt myself lucky to be studying poetry, English novelists and Shakespeare's plays with her.

Intellectually, I was on fire, but I was alone with my blaze. I tried to form an after-school club to discuss the Great Books, and I put posters for the club all over the school. The afternoon of our planned first meeting, I sat in the library with my list of suggested readings. I eagerly watched the door to see which classmates would arrive first. My friend Dennis came in to check out a book on jazz. He carefully avoided my eyes. Two other boys showed up for punitive study hall time. I kept waiting and making excuses for my tardy friends. I found it impossible to believe that students wouldn't jump at the chance to study Thucydides. Finally, the kindly librarian said it was time to lock up. Much to my humiliation, she offered to read one of the Great Books with me.

After that, I kept my thoughts about Pasternak's *Dr. Zhivago* or Ayn Rand's *Atlas Shrugged* to myself. I knew better than to share how many new vocabulary words I had learned that week or how interested I was in the derivation of words. I was already enough of an outcast.

Also, I kept quiet about the fact that, after school, I walked a few blocks to a walled convent for Latin lessons. My mother felt that it was important to know Latin, and she paid for my lessons. I sat with four Catholic students in a cold room with a high ceiling and narrow dusty windows. An elderly nun in a long gray habit taught us conjugations. I enjoyed the quiet immensely, and I found Latin with its soft, round sounds and precise order to be beautiful.

All through high school, I remained shy and especially afraid of boys. My brother Jake warned me about how boys talked about girls in the locker room, which further frightened me. Once, a bully named Arnie put a wood screw on my desk and snickered, "Hey, Mary, do you wanna screw?" I innocently picked it up and said thank you. In study hall one day, another boy drew a picture of what I supposedly looked like naked. He passed it around after making sure that I had seen it. My stomach hurt so much I had to go home early.

Until I was thirteen, I wasn't terribly anxious about my own appearance. That changed the night I watched my first Miss America pageant at a friend's house. As we watched young women dance, twirl batons or walk across the stage in high heels and swimsuits, my friend kept commenting on the girls' legs, tiny waists or nose shapes. I realized I didn't look like any of the young women onstage and that I would never match what appeared to be the feminine ideal. I told my friend that and she didn't disagree. After that I didn't feel pretty.

When I envision high school in Concordia, I see a swirl of actions—playing clarinet in marching band, cheering in Pep Club at our Friday night football games, swimming at the sandpit, baking cookies with my friends, biking to nearby towns, attending slumber parties, or watching Debbie Reynolds, Doris Day and Elvis movies on Saturday nights at the Grand Theater. I can picture myself in my bedroom dancing to records by Harry Belafonte and Peter, Paul and Mary, and the soundtracks of my favorite musicals—*Flower Drum Song, Camelot, Oklahoma!, South Pacific,* and *West Side Story.*

In high school, I worked as a carhop and later as kitchen manager at the A&W drive-in on Highway 81. Taking orders, serving pork tenderloin sandwiches and root beer floats, and collecting money, I learned to deal with cranky, persnickety, lecherous and drunk people. I saw neglected and fearful children who sat in the backseat of cars empty-handed while their parents ate banana splits, and I visited with old people who carefully counted out pennies to pay for their small dishes of soft-serve. Waitressing was great training for my later work as a therapist.

I began to sort out how people were different and how they were the same. I never believed that some people were better than others. That seemed both counterintuitive and unfair. My own experience was that all people—including my family and myself—possessed virtues and vices as mixed as prairie grasses. Also, my relationship with animals was such that I was not inclined to privilege the human race, let alone the white, Christian, rural demographic that was mine.

Living in Kansas, I rarely pondered the issue of race. My dad was from the South, and he had traditional southern views on race. Yet he had socialized with black men during his years in the military and he had liked and respected them. My mother didn't group people by race, gender, religion or income. She divided people into two categories: those who needed her help and those who didn't.

My first despicable experience of racism came in the 1950s when our family was vacationing on Padre Island in Texas. I caught a small fish I couldn't recognize, and I asked an older man who was crabbing nearby if my fish was edible. He answered, "Not for white people." At first, I didn't even understand what he meant. But when I grasped the meaning of his words, I picked up my pole and walked off the dock. I wanted to beat that guy up.

In the towns where I grew up, almost everyone was white and

Protestant. To many people of that time in that place, even Catholics were suspect. There was a great deal of talk about the importance of never dating a Catholic. Sweet Christian ladies talked about "Jewing people down," "Indian giving" or "being gypped." I couldn't understand how people could dislike Jews, Catholics or African-Americans. They didn't know any of these people well enough to hate them.

I was largely ignorant myself until I read *To Kill a Mockingbird, Up from Slavery, Black Like Me,* and *The Autobiography of Malcolm X.* Only in 2008 did I learn that George Washington Carver had graduated from high school in a town thirty miles from Concordia. My father once said of him, "George Washington Carver found a hundred uses for the peanut, but the South never found one use for George Washington Carver." Remembering that now, I wonder what my father thought of the man.

My ways of understanding the world came more from my mother than my father. Avis was more like a wise teacher than a parent. I didn't tell her my troubles, but we did share thoughts about the world. She could find the kernel of meaning in any interaction, and she had an eagle eye for the significant. Everything she said became a parable or a fable. She was the kind of person who could turn the nursery rhyme "Who Killed Cock Robin?" into a treatise on group responsibility.

She struggled to understand the motives and points of view of other people, and she shared her insights with me. For example, one day a man who had accidentally been sprayed with insecticide by a crop duster came in and sat quietly in her office in his poison-soaked clothes. He asked for a visit with Dr. Bray when she had time. The nurse inquired if it was an emergency, and he replied, "I

can wait my turn." He sat politely in the waiting room until the
last patient had been seen. Then he blacked out and crashed to the
floor. My mom saved him and said later, "He is the kind of decent
fellow who would rather die than be presumptuous."

Once during a blizzard, when the roads were closed and the
power was out, my mother asked Dad to carry oxygen tanks
from her clinic to the home of a woman in acute respiratory distress. He trudged through deep snow all night filling one canister,
returning to pick up an empty one and walking it back to the clinic
for a refill. When my mother spoke proudly of Dad the next day,
she said, "Morality is action, not empty words about goodness
and love."

My mother loved what I call crucible stories. Over and over she
recounted tales of Marie Antoinette, the *Titanic*, Scott's polar ex-
peditions and the Russian Revolution, especially the assassination
of Tsar Nicholas and his family. She told me the story about the
death from cancer of John Gunther, Jr., and later bought me his
father's book *Death Be Not Proud*. She also narrated plots of her
favorite movies, one of which was *Dark Victory*. In it, a privileged,
spoiled woman finds love and then goes blind. She becomes a different person as she suffers, and in the end makes a heroic decision. She decides to die alone and in pain so that her doctor husband
can attend an important medical conference.

Avis was fascinated by stories of what people did when their
backs were up against the wall. She felt the choices people make in
those moments reveal their true character. She was a student of
courage, steadfastness and endurance, all characteristics she possessed. Her stories became the bedrock for my moral education. As
a doctor and child of poverty, she had an essentially tragic outlook

on life, but she didn't let that excuse her or anyone from behaving honorably.

Looking back, I think the most sensible decision I made in childhood was to, whenever I could, Velcro myself to my mother. She didn't give me what most mothers give their daughters, but she gave me something else: an education in character.

As a high school graduation present, my parents told me they would take me on a trip to any city I wanted to visit. I chose San Francisco, which delighted them. They loved the Bay Area and thought I wanted to go there because of their stories from the war. In fact, I wanted to go because I had read about beatniks. An older friend, already in college, had told me to check out City Lights bookstore and a café called Coffee and Confusion. My folks bought the plane tickets and reserved a hotel near Union Square.

I deeply regret my adolescent behavior on that trip. My folks wanted to take me to Muir Woods, Alcatraz and their favorite Armenian restaurant. I dreamed of meeting a poet. I wanted to spend every minute in North Beach. Even though I was still wearing puffed sleeves and bobby socks, I considered myself too cool to be escorted around town by a dowdy, middle-aged couple from Kansas. Our different ideas about the trip came to a head the night we went to Coffee and Confusion. I was entranced by the long-haired, barefoot waiter who, to my naïve eyes, looked like Jesus. I fell in love with him and with the grimy but sincere folk singer strumming his guitar onstage.

After a long wait and a few quizzical looks, our waiter approached us for our drink orders. My parents asked for martinis, which, of course, the coffeehouse didn't serve. I was so embarrassed by this I insisted we leave immediately. Dad couldn't figure out what upset me, and I wouldn't tell him. I would give anything now to alter my behavior and relive that trip with my parents who, for once, were trying to show me a good time.

As a child, I lived surrounded by an amazing cast in a continuous drama. I drank in the world. My heart swelled with emotions all the time. With my imagination and my sense for drama, every day I experienced my own personal *Aïda.*

With my peers I felt weak and strange, but with my family I felt strong. If a decision about family activities came up, my dad would say, "Ask Mary. She knows what to do." My uncle Otis once told me, "You handled everything for your family from the time you were seven on."

Even though I had great responsibilities and limited power, I managed to cope. I didn't give up or allow myself to hate anyone. I sought calmness and safety, and usually I could find those things for myself. I lived in the world of books, animals, swimming pools and starry nights. It never occurred to me to feel sorry for myself. Indeed, I felt I was the luckiest child in my family. I enjoyed almost a year with my mother before she began medical school, and I spent the most time with my father before he left for the war. I was rarely punished. I was a love-seeking girl, and for the most part I found love wherever I went.

I realize that my parents made many mistakes and bad decisions. They were remarkably ignorant or indifferent to the needs of us children. They raised their family in a different time, but still, most parents of their era were more competent. They didn't punish their children as severely as my father punished us. They didn't leave children unattended or send them away for a year at a time.

Because I needed to love my parents and to believe they loved me, I couldn't afford to be angry with them. I focused on the good times we had and the attention they did offer me. The words "neglect" and "abuse" were not part of the vocabulary of the times, but even if they had been, I would never have applied them to my family. My mother was a respected doctor and my dad was well liked by almost everyone. I played the glad game.

In order to feel some sense of control, I held myself responsible for everything. It was my job to soothe my parents, and to make sure my brothers and sister were safe. When things went wrong in the family, I didn't blame my parents but, rather, I blamed myself. As a child and even as an adult, I found this way of viewing the world worked for me. Not perfectly, but okay. Only when I became well known did it become a real problem.

If I were a person who bothered with wishing, I might wish that my father hadn't been so hotheaded and restless, and that my mother could have kept me with her when I was five. I would wish my father hadn't been sent to Korea when my brothers and I were so young, that my grandma Glessie hadn't suffered her heart attack when I was eight, that my other grandparents hadn't died so soon after my father's stroke. I would wish my parents were alive and healthy today, enjoying their grandchildren and great-grandchildren.

But I don't waste time wishing. We don't get to tinker with our lives. Ultimately, they are what they are. Besides, there is a sense in which all the people and circumstances of my life created the person I am today. Too much adversity can shut down a soul, but a certain amount of difficulty schools people in resilience. The luckiest children are those who experience challenges, deal properly with them and become more resilient. I didn't have a comfortable childhood, but I had a growth-producing childhood. I had many opportunities to learn and to have fun, and I received a great deal of love and kindness. Nobody gets everything.

LOST AND FOUND
(1965–1977)

In 1965, at seventeen, right after I graduated from high school, I moved to Lawrence and participated in a Summer Honors Institute at the University of Kansas. Lawrence was a beautiful town that had been a center of progressive ideas since the days of Bleeding Kansas in the 1850s, when neighboring Missouri was a slave state and many Kansans wanted to be a free state.

My first night away at college, I stayed up all night talking to Janice, my new roommate. She was a scholarship student from a working-class family in Kansas City. Sitting cross-legged on our twin beds, we discussed books, music, our families and our thoughts about God. She was a liberal, the first I had met among my peers. Her boyfriend had been expelled from high school for refusing to salute the flag and had applied for conscientious objector status because of the war in Vietnam. When I told her I was a Goldwater fan, she laughed.

I felt so lucky to discover a friend of the heart. That summer, I met many more students who had been the bookworms and eggheads at their schools. I felt a great sense of joy at finding my own kind. And I was shocked to discover that boys thought I was attractive. When I got to college, I was asked out all the time. Every day on campus I felt prettier, more confident and less alone. I was no longer the only person in a room who had read all of Dostoyevsky, who liked Harry Belafonte or who questioned racism.

In the fall of my freshman year, I moved into Corbin Hall, a women's dorm that enforced strict rules and required us to dress formally with gloves for Sunday night dinner. Other girls protested the tenets of in loco parentis, but I found it oddly comforting. My life was changing so rapidly that I liked the protections of no-men-beyond-the-lobby and midnight curfews. I loved walking to class on a campus with stately green trees. I spent hours studying in the stacks of the majestic library and attending lectures in rooms with high ceilings and crown molding.

My parents had insisted I take premedicine classes, and even though I loved literature more than anything else, I enrolled in chemistry and biology classes. Long before college, I had buried my dreams of being a writer. I believed that English majors couldn't make a living, and I convinced myself that I had no talent. All through college, I avoided creative writing courses because I felt I would only embarrass myself.

Still, the course catalog was like a Christmas present to me. Soon I was slipping in classes in drama, linguistics, French and the history of Tibet. After a year, and much to the dismay of my parents, I switched majors to Spanish and Latin-American studies. In the 1960s, studying Central America was an education in American power and politics. Small, struggling countries were controlled by the United Fruit Company and by dictators trained at the School of the Americas in Georgia. Tribal societies were vanishing in a wave of colonialism and globalization. Cultural anthropology gave me an insider's understanding of cultures even as they were being transformed. My studies and peers radicalized me, and I rapidly discarded my conservative political attitudes.

In high school, I never smoked, drank, swore or spent much time with anyone who did. In college, I quickly lost my purity and naïveté. Every night I listened to the escapades of Rhonda, a resident assistant, who gave blow jobs on her many dates. She explained that because she was a strong Catholic and wanted to remain a technical virgin, oral sex was her only recourse. The concept of a blow job was almost beyond my ability to understand, but Rhonda's explanations were riveting.

Students from St. Louis and Chicago talked about peyote and mescaline, words I had never even heard. A fraternity boy named Ken Gland, who wanted a career in hotel management, bestowed upon me my first real kiss. Later, when he asked me if I wanted a hickey, I had to admit I didn't know what that was.

Ken and I were fans of the Teepee, a tavern outside town where we danced and drank 3.2 beer. We rocked to "Louie, Louie," "Hang on Sloopy" and "In the Midnight Hour" with the best of the dancers. I loved to sway, toss my long hair around and stand with Ken's arm around my waist and chat with other couples. Finally, I knew how to dance, make out and drink alcohol without coughing.

Soon Ken became boring and conservative for me. I veered toward the campus radicals and artists. With them I dove into everything—art galleries, lectures at the student union, hootenannies and the hip bars with jukeboxes that played Otis Redding, James Brown and Aretha Franklin. I attended films by Cocteau, Bergman and Fellini at the university theater. At the Fiery Fur-

nace, I met my new beatnik pals to drink thick coffee and listen to
bongo drummers and anguished poets reading their dark works
about America, war and their own mental health.

When a group of us rode from Lawrence to Lincoln in the back
of a pickup truck for a Bob Dylan concert, I met my first serious
boyfriend. Larry was a political science major and union organizer
at the box factory where he worked. He was tall, with black hair
and pale skin, and wore industrial boots. Because he did physical
labor, his biceps bulged impressively under his denim work shirts.
Larry called himself a socialist and declared that Dionne Warwick
was the queen of the universe. We listened to blues in smoky bars
in Kansas City and walked along the Kaw River outside Lawrence.
He introduced me to jazz, Surrealist poetry and his union heroes—
Joe Hill, Bill Haywood, Eugene Debs and Woody Guthrie.

Larry gently escorted me into adulthood with his wise discourse
and good questions. He told me I was pretty and lovable, words
I very much needed to hear. He accompanied me to Concordia,
where he found my family, with all its shouting and disorder, upsetting. Afterward he asked me, "Why aren't you angrier?" I
couldn't really answer him. I didn't know myself well enough to
understand that I directed all my anger inward.

Larry wanted to take care of me, and he promised he would
never abandon me or hurt me in any way. He kept his promise and
was a wonderful first partner. Had I been older and more settled, I
might have married him. As it was, I was wild and adventurous,
with absolutely no interest in lifelong commitments. I was just beginning to explore the world.

Our gang of friends feted Allen Ginsberg and his companion,
Peter Orlovksy, when they came to town, and we attended concerts by Odetta, Jean Redpath and Pete Seeger. Standing on the

picnic tables of the Lawrence city parks, we recited poetry and
made proclamations about social justice and peace. We spent
nights drinking red wine around campfires at Lone Star Lake.
Over coffee in the mornings, we talked about our government and
our parents, the Communists, and the fraternity boys, whom we
held in great scorn.

Larry and I joined other students in marches to support inte-
gration in Kansas City and to protest the expanding Vietnam War.
The lofty rhetoric at demonstrations inspired me to learn more,
and soon I was reading Regis Debray, Che Guevara and Frantz
Fanon. When I worked for peace and justice, I felt alive and hopeful. Like many of my peers, I had faith we would remake the
world.

Men were in charge in the 1960s. The women's movement hadn't
come to Kansas, and feminine women kept quiet. In public, Larry
was the leader and I was the pretty, demure girlfriend. The women
made spaghetti or chili for the men, who planned demonstrations.
We listened around the edges of the room and noted that many of
these campus radicals who celebrated freedom thought that their
own girlfriends belonged only in bed or in the kitchen. Still, I was
too content to be much of a feminist.

During my sophomore year in college, my father had his first
massive stroke. I spent my Christmas vacation at a rehabilitation
center in Denver trying to teach him to speak. When I returned to
school and to Larry, I worried a great deal about my mother's burdens and my siblings' loneliness. I have almost no memory of the
rest of that school year. I lived my days in shock and grief.

I also lost both of my grandparents while I was at KU. Grandpa
Page died of a heart attack in his garden while he was burying the
garbage to fertilize his vegetables. I rode with my family to the

funeral in Flagler. The service was in the small church he and my grandmother had helped establish. He was interred with Masonic honors in a prairie cemetery near the old homestead. My grandmother wore her gold dress from their fiftieth wedding anniversary. When I asked her why she didn't wear black, she said, "Fred always liked this dress."

Shortly after his death, my grandmother was diagnosed with leukemia. I visited her the winter she was widowed and dying. She never spoke of her illness but, rather, asked about me. When I expressed my admiration for how brave and uncomplaining she was, she looked at me hard and said, "Look, I am going to be uncomfortable and die soon no matter how I act. I might as well behave with dignity."

On that visit I asked her if she had lived a happy life. She didn't even answer me. I asked her again and she grimaced and replied sharply, "Mary, I don't think of my life that way. I ask, Have I made good use of my time and talents? Is the world a better place because I lived?" I was chastened by her reply and I determined to evaluate my life as she evaluated hers. She was and still is my North Star. Following her guiding light has led me to behave honorably and kindly. However, I never learned to ask the question, "Am I happy?"

After two years at KU, I broke up with Larry and transferred to the University of California. At the time, I told myself it was because I was restless and wanted to be where the best anthropologists taught. Now I see that I was running away from a great deal of pain. After my father's stroke, my family stopped functioning as a unit. My siblings effectively had no parents—one was brain-damaged and the other worked all the time. My biological brothers and sister were adolescents.

After I left for college, my parents adopted two Korean girls from Holt Orphanage. Since his time in Korea, my father had always been interested in the children of that country, and as we children grew older, he convinced my mother that they could handle more children. At the time of his stroke, my two Korean sisters were just beginning elementary school. Jane had been in our family for a year, but Kim had been in this country only five months. Both badly needed parental attention and guidance, and instead they were left very much to fend for themselves in a traumatized family.

I could have done more for them and for my biological siblings, but I couldn't bear to go home and see all the misery. The great allure of California was partly that it was far away. To this day, I am not sure how much I was running toward a good life or running away from an unbearable one.

I enrolled at UC Santa Barbara, but eventually I moved to Berkeley, where the action was. Just as the Bay Area was my mother's Mecca, it soon became mine. My brother Jake moved to San Francisco around that time. We spent a lot of time visiting each other and enjoying the best of both Berkeley and San Francisco.

At the University of California, I walked to class across Sproul Plaza by the Administration Building where all the speeches and protests were held. Berkeley was a lively place, with reggae bands, topless girls selling tacos and men handing out flyers about free love or Black Power. Once, when I was walking to campus along Telegraph Avenue, I saw in a shop window a satiny black dress covered with shiny tassels. It barely covered my behind and cost twenty-five dollars. I sold my blood to buy it.

I roomed with students from Boston and New York and developed a scrim of sophistication. We lived in a commune where we

traded books and records. I hung posters of Marlon Brando and Albert Einstein in my little room. I owned a ratty fur coat, a brass bed
and heaps of paperbacks and anthropology textbooks. As I visited
clubs in North Beach and participated in "happenings" in Golden
Gate Park and on Mount Tamalpais, my musical taste evolved
from the Everly Brothers and Peter, Paul and Mary, to Country
Joe and the Fish, Mose Allison and Janis Joplin. I danced at the
Fillmore and the Avalon to the Grateful Dead, Jefferson Airplane
and the Chambers Brothers. Every day of my life was "trippy."
My head was exploding.

At our commune, we ate brown rice and local organic vegetables with our alfalfa tea and jug wine. As the most industrious of
our house members, I did a lot of sweeping, cooking and washing
dishes. Weekdays, I wore faded jeans, dangly earrings, high-heeled
sandals and a khaki army jacket. On Saturday nights, I ironed my
long blond hair, put on my sexy black dress and wore a pink and
gold scarf from India as a headband. I fell in love with musicians,
revolutionaries and poets.

In college and during my twenties, I explored spiritual beliefs
from all over the world. For a brief time, I majored in religious stud-
ies, surveying the world's religions with great interest. I resonated
with both the Greek Orthodox Church and the Tibetan Buddhists.
Books by Carlos Castaneda, Alan Watts, and George Gurdjieff, and
Hermann Hesse's *Siddhartha*, Ram Dass's *Be Here Now* and John
Neihardt's *Black Elk Speaks* became my sacred texts. Soon I was
reading astrological charts, and interpreting tarot cards and the I
Ching for my friends. To celebrate the summer solstice, I danced
Sufi dances beside Half Moon Bay. At the Open University, I
signed up for a class called "Howling at the Moon."

Mainly, I drank wine on rooftops and beaches and listened to my friends talk about their experiences. Some of my friends took LSD as a way to understand God. Others had spent time in Esalen or India. My curiosity was more anthropological than spiritual. I liked to hear all the ways we humans could describe God to ourselves.

Some of my friends experimented with drugs as a form of prayer. They wanted to open themselves to the universe and feel closer to God. I tried peyote and marijuana, but I didn't enjoy them. They left me jittery, suspicious and fragile. I can't blame all these feelings on drugs. I felt that way a good share of the time, but drugs only heightened my self-consciousness and anxiety. I've seen a bumper sticker, "Reality is for people who can't handle drugs." I was one of those people.

I don't want to imply I was a carefree flower child. My last semester at Berkeley, I protested the university's razing of People's Park. Thousands of students demonstrated to stop the university from turning what was a beautiful community garden into a parking lot. I learned some hard lessons in what our government does to troublemakers. The manager of the film theater was shot and killed while watching the protests from the roof of his apartment building. Some of my friends were arrested, badly beaten and emotionally shaken by their time in police custody. Walking to class, I was sickened by the tear gas dropped from helicopters. In the end, the park was surrounded by a big fence and destroyed.

I also denied my pain and fear of the future. I kept my anxiety and guilt about leaving my family to myself. No matter how exciting my life was, I knew that I was far from home while my father struggled to recover from his first stroke. Jake and I could emotionally support each other, but I knew my mother and my other siblings missed me. In retrospect, I can see that I was maturing and

adrift, and ecstatic and sorrowful. I felt myself to be some combination of Simone de Beauvoir and Judas Iscariot. My mind was
racing so rapidly away from who I had been that I felt a chronic
mental vertigo. I didn't choose to examine what was churning inside me. When I received my degree in anthropology in 1969, I
knew more about the Zulus and the Trobriand Islanders than I did
about myself.

By the time I graduated, I had lived in many places with many
different kinds of people. At twenty-one, I never wanted to settle
down. I couldn't afford graduate school and I considered being a
waitress forever. Money meant nothing to me, and I liked talking
to people as I served them food. Yet my first job after graduation
was at a department store on Union Square in San Francisco. I was
in training to be a buyer of ethnic goods from foreign markets.
Wearing nylons and sitting in a cubicle on a sunny San Francisco
day was torture to me. I lasted for two weeks before I cashed my
first paycheck and hitchhiked with a friend to Mexico.

We rented a small cabana on the beach and lived for the summer on tortillas, shrimp and oranges. When we ran low on books, we
exchanged what we had with other Americans. For three months,
I swam every day and watched the sun rise and set. I spoke Spanish with the locals and soon had a passable accent. After three
months, I was tired of paradise and almost out of money, so I decided to use the last of my savings for a trip to Europe.

I bought a plane ticket on Icelandic to London and set off with
a hundred dollars in my pocket. I stopped in Kansas on my way.
My mother was overworked and solemn, and my siblings seemed
lonely, needy and confused. Partially blind, and paralyzed on one
side of his body, my father sat on the couch in the living room.

Even though his language was limited, I could tell that he didn't approve of my short skirts, headband or politics. Dad didn't know exactly what I was up to, but he had a strong sense it was no damned good. Even so, I felt that my presence gave him, my mother and my siblings a great deal of support and pleasure. Still, I didn't stay. I left for a year in London, reassuring myself that my letters would be sufficient.

I left because America scared me and I had no idea what to do next. Our country was at war and deeply divided on almost every important social issue. The National Guard was killing college students on their campuses. Our leaders were lying to us. Innocent people far away were being slaughtered in our country's name. As my friends dropped out of society or became increasingly radicalized, I felt more and more alienated from everyone. I have never been a good hater, and I am uncomfortable with divisiveness. I don't like us–them thinking. At my core, I have always known that there is no "us" and no "them."

I didn't fit anywhere. The Bay Area had grown violent with hard drugs and guns. I couldn't see myself living in my hometown and blending in with my high school friends. By the fall of 1969, I could no longer handle the clamor and intensity. So I ran away.

In many ways, England was a good choice. Compared with the United States, it was a relaxed, nonpolarized place. Even though I didn't have a work permit, I found employment easily. All my life, I have been offered jobs on the spot by business owners who noticed how quickly I could write out a check or connect socially with the people around me. In London, I worked at both a Jewish bakery and a cinema. I survived on challah and fish and chips.

In England, I gave myself a break from politics and lost myself in other centuries. I read Trollope, Austen, Dickens and John Stuart Mill. I toured museums, castles and other historic sites, and I attended meetings of the H. G. Wells Society.

Although I felt lonely, I steered clear of emotional entanglements. Quite correctly, I discerned that I needed to sort myself out with no one influencing me. Still, after a few months, I grew depressed and yearned for my family. I was not and have never been someone who can live far from people I love.

Christmas Eve in London was dreadful. I walked into a party held by some friends of an acquaintance in the States. The place was small but elegant, with Miles Davis on the record player and a table set with linen napkins and fine crystal. The hosts were friendly, but raucous and not particularly interested in getting to know me. The man who sat beside me at dinner kept trying to feel me up. Finally, I slapped his hand loudly and told him to cut it out. I was as red as the beets on the table, but everyone laughed as if his rudeness was a joke.

As I sat in the midst of strangers who were getting drunk and telling dirty stories, I envisioned my family sitting around a tree in our snowy Kansas town. My siblings would be missing me even as they opened gifts and played cards. My dad would be sitting on the couch drinking coffee and watching the party. My tired mother would be yearning for me as she sliced a pecan pie and later washed dishes. I felt guilt and rage at myself for my foolish choices.

By the time I returned to Kansas six months later, I was broke, anemic and worn out. After thinking seriously about my future, I decided to move back to Lawrence and finish the courses I needed for the premed major I had begun years earlier. That fall, I applied and was accepted to medical school in Kansas City. Pending the completion of my premed classes, I was in for the next summer. I was ready for a stable life, one in which I could be useful and make an adequate income.

Something else happened that year. Back in Kansas, I became pregnant with a man whom I decided not to marry. That dark winter of my pregnancy, as I struggled with the emotional and practical issues of having a child, my friends in Kansas City saved me. Poor, embarrassed and frightened for my future, I couldn't have remained in college without their financial and emotional support. Until Zeke was born, I had a room in a candle-making commune in a neighborhood where old trees canopied the streets.

The Christmas I was pregnant, my mother didn't allow me to come home. She wanted to protect my three younger sisters from my bad influence, and she didn't relish me walking around downtown with a big belly and no ring. I wasn't angry with her for this decision. Rather, I agreed that I deserved her censure, and I felt great remorse that I had caused her even more misery than she was already enduring. However, I felt fragile and sad. The previous Christmas I'd been in London, and now, even though I was in Kansas, I couldn't see my family.

To cheer me up, my friends in the commune prepared a vegetarian feast and gave me practical gifts for the baby. As I laughed and joined in the carol singing, I ached to be home helping my mother fix turkey and playing dominoes and Monopoly with my siblings. I felt the way I did the year I lived in a trailer in the Ozarks: banished.

Just before Zeke's birth, a close friend and I moved into a small apartment near the Country Club Plaza. Laura worked as a waitress at the nearby Chinese restaurant, House of Toy. Every night she would bring us delicious leftovers. We survived that spring on garlic chicken and egg foo yong. When I wasn't studying, Laura and I had long talks and plenty of laughter. Our relationship helped me weather an icy season.

During the week, I studied physics and organic chemistry at the University of Missouri, and on weekends, I went with my friends to the Nelson-Atkins Museum of Art or the Vanguard Coffee House, where Steve Martin opened one night for the Nitty Gritty Dirt Band with his magic tricks.

On a Friday night, the week before spring break, after a hearty meal of Peking duck, I went into labor. I called the kind doctor who treated me free of charge, and I called my mother, who said she was on her way. Laura and I rode the bus to the hospital. After a night of hard labor, with Laura and my mother by my side, Zeke was born at sunrise. I still don't have words to write about that experience. The minute I held Zeke for the first time was the happiest moment of my life. From the beginning, I was madly in love with my blue-eyed son.

My mother bought me roses and fresh fruit. My friends came to visit and admire my son. The sun pouring into the hospital room warmed Zeke and me.

After Zeke was born, my mother welcomed us back to her home. With her typical cavalier attitude toward children's development, she offered to raise Zeke for me until I finished medical school in five years. That idea horrified me. I could hardly bear to part with Zeke for a second. I would not repeat history. I dropped out of medical school before my summer classes began. Never for a minute have I regretted that decision.

Single mothers were not common in that time and place. When people asked me about Zeke's father, I blushed and said I was not married, then quickly moved on to other topics. For several years after Zeke was born, I avoided my aunts and uncles because I couldn't bear to face them as a fallen woman. In Concordia, my family was kind to Zeke and me, but I felt embarrassed and judged in my hometown. I was once again the talked-about outsider.

However, all of that was tempered by my pride in my son. How could I feel ashamed of an event that produced someone so magnificent? Zeke's presence in the world redeemed whatever mistakes I had made. Taking good care of him had the inadvertent effect of helping me take better care of myself. I settled down and began to make better decisions about relationships, time and money. We became a small, contented family of two.

When Zeke was eighteen months old, I enrolled in graduate school in psychology at the University of Nebraska. I had hoped to go to graduate school in anthropology, but I couldn't afford that. I had a baby to support and no savings. Psychology became an attractive alternative when I learned that I could receive full funding while I worked on a doctorate.

My surprise admission to this program occurred because of one conversation I had with a kind professor. After hearing I would not receive a stipend in the anthropology department, I walked by the psychology office and decided to drop in. Even though I had never taken psychology courses, Dr. Cole invited me to sit down and visit with him.

We talked about my anthropology training and my travels, my father's stroke and my earnest, but grandiose, interest in a unified field theory for human behavior. I showed him a paper I had written on that topic. He read a few pages and asked about my college grades. Then he said I was welcome to enter the program. Since I had never taken any psychology classes, I needed to enroll in a few courses before the fall program began. I could start summer school the next week. I will always be grateful for Dr. Cole's professional support. Because of it, I could continue my education and Zeke could be in university day care.

Once again I was back on my home turf, a college campus. Zeke and I quickly made friends with the faculty and my classmates. Psychologists tend to be nurturers, talkers and empathetic listeners— perfect friends for me. We nestled into a community that for five years helped us both grow up. I loved those years of study and parenting. On the weekends, Zeke and I would visit the natural history museum or the Children's Zoo. I read him a million books and taught him to play Slap Jack and dominoes.

While I couldn't dance, sing, work with my hands or tolerate the dullness of numbers, I was a natural for psychology. My main skills were communicating, empathizing and connecting. I was deeply curious about other people's points of view, and I liked to unravel questions about motive and character structure. Doing therapy seemed as natural as breathing. Being a therapist was not so different from being a waitress in a small town. Both were fine ways to explore the human heart.

There was one hitch: I was expected to teach. Since I had never spoken in class or in any kind of group since my earlier traumas, I was terrified at the thought of giving a lecture. To make my situation even more alarming, I was assigned to a human sexuality class. Not only would I be standing in front of three hundred undergraduates, but also I would be talking to them about penises and vaginas, orgasms, homosexuality and what we then called "social diseases."

My first day of teaching I was so nervous I could barely walk onto the dais in front of my class. My legs wobbled, my throat felt dry and constricted, and I couldn't quite catch my breath. Exceedingly shy and only a few years older than my students, I lit a cigarette to steady myself. I rasped out a greeting, then my voice cleared and I felt more comfortable. Launching into my lecture, I felt almost confident until I noticed that I had two cigarettes going. I blushed, stubbed one out and kept on talking.

I met Jim my first day in graduate school. He was tall, big-boned and good-looking, and he wore the same denim work shirts and blue jeans that my first serious boyfriend, Larry, had favored. Only Jim wore them with cowboy boots. We were friends right away. He helped me with statistics class and departmental politics. Because I stayed up late to study after Zeke went to bed and woke early to play with him, I was inclined to fall asleep in class. Jim would poke me under the table to wake me up before I alienated my professors. As we grew closer, we vowed never to date; it would make our graduate school years too complicated.

At first, it was easy for us to keep that vow. Jim played in several bands and hoped to become a professional musician with a life on the road. Psychology was his "fallback career." I was engrossed with caring for Zeke and my coursework. During the years I attended graduate school, at different times my father, my brother John and my sister Toni each moved to Lincoln to be near me.

Jim and I kept our vows to be friends until about Christmas of our first year in graduate school. Then, one night after studying late, we confessed we had romantic feelings for each other. I am not sure why Jim fell for me, but I know why I fell for him. I liked his sense of humor and absolute decency. He was a good talker and hard worker and, most important, he was kind to Zeke.

We were opposites in many ways. Jim was raised in a small Nebraska town founded by Piphers. His father was city attorney and seemed related to everyone. His mother was a home economics major who wore beautiful clothes and elaborate jewelry. Jim's family was well organized, predictable and prosperous. Their house was elegant, quiet and tidy. Phyllis served the same healthy breakfast every morning. In fact, she set the breakfast table each night before bed. I had never experienced anything like that.

From day one, Jim couldn't believe the amount of activity and strangeness that existed in my life. He'd come by to pick me up for class and discover Zeke in his underwear eating dried cuttlefish and shrimp chips as he watched me interpret an I Ching reading for friends from California with names like Sparkle and Elf.

When Jim and I first dated, my parents and three sisters were still in Concordia. John had joined Jake in San Francisco. Jim, Zeke and I would walk into my parents' house to find my mother cooking, my dad sitting on the couch smoking and my two youngest sisters running around half dressed. Unread magazines and newspapers and unopened bills cascaded off the tables, and piles of clean but not folded laundry piled up on the couches and chairs. Usually both the television and the record player were blaring, the phone was ringing and a neighbor was dropping by with some elderberries, which my mom would make into jelly, or maybe some mountain oysters, which my dad liked to fry up. The place was always in a state of what Jim called "maximum hectosity."

Once, when we visited my parents, Jim noticed the house was dark inside. He changed one lightbulb, and then he noticed another. He twice drove to a store for more lightbulbs and ended up changing twenty of them before he had all the lights working again. He said ruefully of my family, "It is as if whenever your parents enter a room, they scatter chaos dust all over the place."

When Jim and I studied for our comprehensives in psychology, I was struck by how different our work styles were. I set to work in January and studied hard until I was ready for the exam. I was a

fast reader and an organized student, and by early April, two weeks
before comps, I was merrily bike riding with my friends. Jim was
a slow reader and a procrastinator. All winter he had been practicing with his bands and watching Johnny Carson and Tom Snyder
on late-night TV. By March, he still had most of his reading to do
and spent every spare minute cramming.

Emotionally we were opposites as well. Jim was as steady and
calm as I was easily rattled and changeable. For every decision, I
was the gas; he was the brakes. I wanted ten children; he was quite
happy with only Zeke. Many years after we married, we had this
interaction: I had terrible insomnia, and after several hours, I woke
Jim to ask him what he thought about in the two minutes it took
him to fall asleep. He said, "Pie." He wasn't joking. Then he asked
me what I was thinking about. I answered, "The Holocaust." That
about sums us up.

In October 1974, we married in Jim's home in Nebraska with
just our two families present. His mother decorated the house with
flowers, a wedding cake and a bachelor cake. She passed flutes of
champagne before the ceremony. My raggedy family was impressed and a little overwhelmed by the elegance.

Jim wore a cowboy shirt and jeans, and I wore a plaid wool suit
that would serve as my professional outfit for the next four years.
Zeke looked sharp in a corduroy cowboy jacket and a shirt with
silver buttons. When it was time for me to make a grand entrance
into the living room, I froze as I often do when I am overwhelmed
by emotion. Jim had to come comfort me, take my hand and lead
me into the room. A woman judge who had attended elementary
school with Jim's father administered our vows.

Afterward, we stood on the front porch and watched Zeke and
his new cousins tumble in the red and gold leaves. Geese honked

overhead in a blue sky. My mother did her best to make small talk. Toni and my brother John embraced me, and Kim and Jane joined in the decorating of our car. My father lit a Kool and told me in his halting language, "This is a good family. Don't mess things up."

Finally, Jim and I drove off in our Pinto, decorated with cans, toilet-paper rolls and "Just Married" soaped on the windows. Jim's parents watched Zeke while we had a one-night honeymoon at the Holiday Inn in Omaha.

Jim and I recently celebrated our anniversary by talking about what had surprised us about each other over the thirty-four years we have been married. I told him I was surprised that he had learned to like vegetables and poetry and that he now reads good literature. He was surprised I had turned out to be so straitlaced. He had married an adventurous hippie only to find himself living with a bird-watching bookworm who goes to bed before nine.

The next August, after we finished our graduate school classes, we had a yard sale and made about a hundred dollars selling everything we owned except our clothes. We drove to Galveston for internships at the University of Texas Medical Center. We lived in a small apartment with almost no furniture. Zeke attended kindergarten nearby. Like my mother at USC, I had a pair of cheap shoes and two dresses that I wore on alternate days. Jim was reduced to wearing some salmon-colored cords his mother had given him years earlier. I was pregnant with Sara, and every morning, as Jim drove us to work along the fishy bayou, I threw up my breakfast. As my stomach grew larger, I did assessments and therapy with the poor and homeless. I worked up until the day before she was born.

The director of the ob-gyn department delivered Sara. Jim was by my side coaching me on breathing. Together we held Sara for the first time. Zeke came to see his little sister after kindergarten. She was a long, skinny baby with olive dark eyes. I had no sick leave or maternity leave on internship, so I took my week's vacation time to be with her. Then I returned to work full-time. Thank goodness our internship ended in five months and we could move back to Nebraska. That was when my roaming ended. At last, I had a family and a home.

Like many people, I found the time between when I left my family of origin and when I formed my own family to be both exhilarating and discouraging. I had many peak experiences—marching for civil rights, watching the moon rise over the Pacific and listening to great musicians in San Francisco clubs. I lived a life of conversations about everything from grandparents to Foucault, Dadaism, Huey Long and the fate of the Franklin Expedition. But I also spent a good deal of time heartbroken, guilty, confused about my relationships and utterly unsure about my future.

During this era, the best things that happened to me were Zeke's birth, graduate school, meeting and marrying Jim, and Sara's birth. By the time I had interesting, useful work and my own family to cherish, I was settled, in the deepest sense of the word. My years as a wife, the mother of young children, and a psychologist were the happiest of my life. At last I had what I had always yearned for—a job caring for others and a family to eat dinner with every night and cook breakfast for every morning.

LOVE AND WORK

(1977–1994)

By the time Jim and I finished graduate school, we were a family of five, counting our black Lab, Hank. We moved from Texas to York, Nebraska, population 8,000, where Jim directed the mental health clinic. His main office was next to a hatchery and feed store. He told his first-time clients to look for the giant red chicken head beside his office. Several days a week, he drove to little towns and saw clients in church basements.

I commuted a hundred miles a day to Lincoln, first to teach psychology at the university and later to work at the community mental health center. In the summer, the drive was past green fields and cattle; but in the winter, I drove through blizzards and on icy roads. One of my travel games was counting the number of cars that had slid into the ditches. Partly to get both of us off the road, Jim and I moved to Lincoln and established a private practice. Jim joined a bluegrass band, and I had more time to enjoy the children.

Since our office was five blocks from our house, I could walk home for lunch and be with the children by five. In that stage of my life, I flourished. Supervising bathing, dressing and tooth-brushing, I had no time to ponder existential questions or analyze myself. I fixed hot chocolate, quesadillas and chicken à la king. Like all moms, I tied shoes and put on snow boots, bought grocer-ies and children's clothing, and drove the kids to dentist appoint-ments and plays. I read the children Dr. Seuss, Shel Silverstein's poetry and the Babar books, and accompanied them to circuses, zoos and the natural history museum: Music lessons, parent-teacher meetings and swim meets kept me happily hopping. On summer nights, as the sun went down and the lightning bugs blinked on, we watched Zeke pitch. I felt rich.

Reading by the fireside, dancing to Jim's band, telling jokes at dinner—that was the life for me. I engineered our picnics, kite flying, bike rides and family parties. On snowy nights, I lay next to Jim and listened to the north wind howling. Knowing the children were tucked into their beds and that we were all safe and warm, I felt such peace. Falling asleep, I would hope for a snow day when we could sled, make snow ice cream and cross-country ski.

When the children were young, we traveled once a year to Vacation Village on Lake Okiboji in Iowa. Jim's family had stayed in the same cabins when he was a boy. We would wake on a sum-mer morning with the clear lake nearby and the birds singing. Af-ter pancakes, we would all head for the beach. While the children built sand castles and swam, I read novels. We would picnic for lunch and the children would enter talent shows or participate in organized treasure hunts or watermelon-eating contests. After they fell asleep in their bunks, Jim and I would sit outside in our lawn chairs. He would play his guitar and sing.

We also traveled frequently with Jim's band, the Bluegrass

Crusade. One year this group played a festival in the Black Hills of South Dakota, which gave our family the opportunity to finance a memorable vacation. As we drove past little towns on our way to Rapid City, we could see Fourth of July fireworks exploding all around us. We camped in a state forest, and while the children slept in our Vanagon camper, Jim and I built a fire and drank brandy as we breathed in the pines and the silence.

We camped in Wind Cave National Park. At dusk, Jim climbed up a hill to see a herd of elk. On his way down, he encountered a small hissing rattlesnake. We looked up from our picnic table to see him leaping like a deer down a hillside. He told us later that he had decided he could walk slowly and carefully down that snake-infested path or take such big jumps that he wasn't much of a target. That incident made for a good campfire story for years to come.

The next day we took the kids to the Plunge, a famous swimming pool that Jim had visited as a boy. We toured Reptile Gardens, where Zeke was selected to tap the alligator and wake it up. We stopped for rock shops and ice cream. On the way home after the festival, we fished all night at Lake McConahey and caught fifty-eight white bass. They glistened silver in the moonlight.

Jim and I had memorable anniversary meals at restaurants such as Bo Ling's in Kansas City, Gaido's in Galveston, the French Café in Omaha or the Soul Food Kitchen in Lincoln. On our road trips, we sought good barbecue and Mexican food. In Lincoln, I joined happily in potlucks, gourmet clubs and cooking adventures. Once, a friend and I made plum sauce from wild Nebraska plums. Another time, we smoked ourselves out of the kitchen trying to prepare blackened redfish.

Our big luxury was music. Even when we were on a tight bud-

get, Jim and I would spring for concert tickets and drive for hours
to see our heroes. We steeped ourselves in music. Over the years,
we have attended concerts by Muddy Waters, Jackson Browne,
George Jones, Greg Brown, Leo Kottke, Willie Nelson, John Prine,
Count Basie, Doc Watson, Townes Van Zandt, Joan Baez, Solomon
Burke, Van Morrison, Ralph Stanley, Lucinda Williams, Ella Fitz-
gerald, Loudon Wainwright and many more. We even splurged
and paid for a camping trip down the Rio Grande with Butch Han-
cock as our river guide and musical entertainment.

I have long believed that happiness is a matter of satisfying
daily, weekly, monthly and yearly routines. Over the years we developed these for ourselves. Our daily routines were built around
meals, work, talks and bird-watching. Saturday mornings I had coffee with my writers' group. Out-of-town friends and family regularly came for visits. In the spring our family canoed the Niobrara
River in the Sandhills, and in the fall we camped along the Platte
River. In March we traveled west to watch the annual crane migration.

At Christmas every year, we attended a potluck banquet and
dance with two hundred friends at Welfare Hall, built by the Ger-
mans from Russia early in the last century. This party, started as a
reunion for the children of Oakland, Nebraska, had expanded over
the years to include the friends of those "children" and the Oakies'
own grown children.

To my mind, Christmas is walking on crunchy snow into the
creaky old hall in the "Russian Bottoms." We walk into the
warmth of the hall with its music, candles and tables laden with
our traditional favorites—pâté, smoked salmon, *ostkaka* and blueberry sour cream pies. With this feast we fend off, for a night, winter, troubles and even tragedies. We are together holding hands

or dancing to "Beer Barrel Polka." We're making toasts, some of them in Swedish, and celebrating our decades of friendship. The lights, the glitter and the voices of my friends turn a dark winter's night into something radiant.

During these years, my spiritual home was the Unitarian Church. The Unitarians believe in the free and responsible search for truth and meaning, and they have a long history of social activism. As my aunt Margaret told me proudly, "Unitarians don't have answers, but we have the best questions."

At least in my town, Unitarians are the wonky eggheads, progressives, gays, the chronically strange, the highly opinionated, the seekers and the deeply tolerant. We tend to view life as a continuing education program. We have in-jokes such as: "Unitarians would rather go to a lecture on heaven than go to heaven itself." "Why do Unitarians sing hymns badly?" "Because they read ahead to make sure they agree with all the words." Unitarians emphasize learning and the development of the human spirit. At last I had found a group who would discuss the Great Books with me.

Except for our years in Texas and rural Nebraska, Jim and I have lived in the same town with the same friends since 1972. Jim still plays music with two of his friends from kindergarten. We belong to various communities—our neighborhood, our psychologist colleagues and our writer and musician friends. I know the librarians, the checkers at my grocery store and the clerks at my local bookstore. In Lincoln, my deep desire to connect to people and feel loved has been fulfilled. Sometime in the late 1970s, I stopped feeling like an oddball.

My own happy family was a corrective emotional experience. Very intentionally, I made different decisions and choices than my parents. Jim and I were child-focused parents who celebrated every birthday, concert, team victory and honor roll report card. I was a teacher's helper at Sara's school and a Cub Scout leader for Zeke's troop. I compensated for my own childhood loneliness by over-nurturing. My children never missed me. Rather, they sometimes wished I would go out more, and they complained I was always asking them how they were feeling.

Just as my family gave me great joy, so did my profession. Jim and I worked with two therapists who were our close friends in a "Small is beautiful" setting. Zeke and Sara cleaned our office on Saturdays for their allowance. Since we wanted plenty of time to be parents and to have fun, we set firm limits on our number of clients. We never had much money, but we weren't consumers. We always chose time over money.

Being a therapist was the perfect job for me in terms of both my talents and interests. I was lucky the two coincided. I was privileged to be able to spend thirty years listening to what people said when I asked, "What brings you in today?" I received a lifelong education in point of view.

As a child, I was desperately eager to predict behavior and understand emotions. I focused on people's feelings to an extraordinary degree. In junior high, I wasn't interested in Sputnik as science, but only about how the cosmonauts felt about leaving their families and being so far from Earth. I wasn't a girl who cared about prom dresses. I was concerned about how my friends *felt* about their prom dresses. I wasn't particularly interested in the details of a disaster, but I cared about the choices people made in extreme circumstances.

People who enter therapy almost always see themselves as in crisis, and I felt deeply honored to help them explore their thoughts and feelings and reach new understandings of their situations. I liked to spend my days talking to people about what mattered to

them. Seeing people in their darkest moments allowed me to participate in their journey toward hope and strength. In the thirty
years I worked as therapist, I was never bored. And coming from
me, that is a strong tribute.

My workdays consisted of six or seven "fifty-minute hours." I
enjoyed one-on-one interactions in which I could forge deep relationships. I took pride and pleasure in making things better for
struggling families. Easing tensions and creating more positive environments for children and adults was a corrective emotional experience for me. I couldn't fix my own family of origin, but I could
help mend other broken families.

Psychology is a helping profession in the deepest sense of the
word. I had great respect for my clients, even love for them. I didn't
see them as different from people not in therapy. Rather, most of
them were simply trying hard to do the right thing and be the best
people they could be.

I developed a deep reverence for the heroism of ordinary people.
One of my clients was a truck driver raising his teenage daughter
in the aftermath of his wife's suicide. Another was a gay teenager
who struggled to respect himself and deal with a hostile family
and school environment. I worked with a stockbroker who cried
for so many months after his wife's death that he almost lost his
job. Over the years, I saw a wife who cared for her husband with
advanced Alzheimer's, and a ten-year-old girl who desperately
wanted to help her mother stop drinking.

The longer I was a therapist, the more aware I was of how basi-
cally good and decent most people are. I observed that nobility
is scattered more or less evenly across all social, racial and eco-
nomic groups. I also learned that everyone is carrying heavy burdens. Everyone.

As best I could in sleepy Nebraska, I continued to work for human rights. I wrote Urgent Action letters for Amnesty International and volunteered at the refugee center for Southeast Asians. I attended trainings in Minneapolis at the Center for Victims of Torture and at Harvard on how to work with victims of torture. Whenever possible, I marched for peace and for the abolition of the death penalty with the same hundred progressives in our state.

I continued to teach part-time at the University of Nebraska and also at Nebraska Wesleyan University. My main courses were clinical and abnormal psychology, but over time I added sex roles and gender, and the psychology of women. Preparing courses, talking to students about ideas and encouraging them to grow intellectually was profoundly satisfying work. As a teacher and as a therapist, I yearned to help people be stronger, go deeper and find more meaningful lives. I couldn't imagine spending my time any other way.

In the 1980s, as my children matured, I had my first discretionary time since graduate school. I didn't want to take on extra therapy clients or clean my house more thoroughly. Pondering what I wanted to do, I realized with a jolt that I wanted to write. I didn't expect to be good at it or to be published, but I realized that, since I had been in elementary school, I had been yearning to write. Finally, I could respect my own deep desire.

I set my clock radio for five a.m. so that I could write for a couple of hours before my workday began. Like most self-taught writers, I read books on writing and attended writers' workshops. Whenever I could, I attended readings. Listening to Richard Russo, Hilda Raz, Carol Bly and Billy Collins inspired me to spend as much time as I could in the world of beautiful language. I helped form a women's writers' group that we christened Prairie Trout.

I signed up for a college course in creative writing. My teacher was an ex-football coach from Texas who played the ponies in his spare time. He was a magnificent writer and teacher. When I visited his office and timidly asked if he thought I could become a writer, he grinned at me and said, "You are already a writer. Work regularly on your skills and soon you'll be ready to roll."

The great gift of my middle years was writing. I loved carrying a coffee cup into my study in the mornings to spend four or five hours writing and thinking. This activity offered me solitude, serenity and stimulation. While writing, I felt challenged and relaxed at the same time. In this sense, writing was like backpacking. From both I emerged completely happy.

Of course, it didn't seem that way at first. As Nebraska author Willa Cather said, "Nobody is good at the beginning." After a buried novel, *Memoirs of a Kansas Beatnik*, and other failed projects, I managed to publish a few short stories and personal essays. Eventually, I discovered I most liked to write about the effects of culture on mental health.

Pete Seeger asked of music, not "Is it good?" but "What is it good for?" His words encouraged me to think about how I could make my writing as educational and empowering as my therapy. How could I help readers feel stronger, calmer and more optimistic? How could my words aid readers in understanding other people? After almost twenty years, I am still wrestling with these questions.

In the late 1980s, I finished a book called *Hunger Pains* about women's relationships to food and their own bodies. Through a friend, writer Kent Haruf, I found a wonderful agent, Susan Lee Cohen. She liked my book but she couldn't sell it.

A few years later, I sent Susan a sixteen-page proposal for *Reviving Ophelia*. After sending it to thirteen editors, she found one who was interested. I signed a contract with Jane Isay at Putnam's in New York. Just after Susan sold my proposal, my mother was hospitalized with heart problems and diabetes. I called my new editor to tell her I couldn't write while my mother was so ill. Jane kindly told me to call her after my mother's troubles were over.

That next year, I drove weekly from Lincoln to Concordia to care for my mother. My sisters came when they could, but they lived far away from Kansas at this time. Of course, I kept teaching, doing therapy and caring for my teenagers; but weekends, and sometimes during the week, I sat by my mother's bedside in the hospital she had worked in for decades. Looking back, I am grateful for every one of our hours together.

When a nurse called to tell me that my mother had died, I was seeing my afternoon therapy clients. My first thought was, "This time I've lost her for good. She won't be coming from Denver to pick me up and move us to a new town."

The day after my mother's funeral, I began writing *Reviving Ophelia*. By then, Zeke was in college and Sara was in high school. My family seemed to be disappearing. Already, Zeke lived across town in a dormitory at Nebraska Wesleyan. Most of the time, Sara was busy with her friends and activities. The house stayed tidy and quiet.

I felt a sense of poignancy—perhaps I should call it heartbreak— about my children leaving home. One day I walked through the children's clothing section of a department store and I broke down sobbing at the thought that I might never buy a sleeper or snow-suit again.

When I contemplated my future without my mother and my children at home, I was so sad I couldn't speak. Sometimes I think my entire professional writing career was my attempt to fill the hollow spaces in my heart that reopened when my mother died and the children left home.

My years as a wife, mother, teacher and therapist were mostly happy ones. Of course, I experienced tragic events, such as the deaths of friends and relatives, as well as the small, everyday tragedies that hurt badly enough at the time. However, I was reasonably resilient. My work and my companions comforted and distracted me from too much worrying. I enjoyed my siblings, my cousins and my aunts and uncles. Walks on Holmes Dam or in Wilderness Park calmed and soothed me. Indeed, my primary attachment may be to the natural world. People have come and gone, but Mother Nature has never abandoned me. Many times over, the color green has mended my aching heart or fading spirit. Books, people and going outdoors have long been my trinity of coping devices.

However, looking back on those years, I can recognize vulnerabilities that I ignored at the time. For example, I had never paid much attention to my health. I almost lost a retina because I didn't bother to have my eyes checked regularly. After I bruised my heart in an auto accident, I carried on as if nothing had happened. I was home picking up socks and toys before I left for work when I felt some chest pain. I held my arm to my chest and kept working until Jim asked what was wrong with me. Had he not been home, I might simply have carried on with my day until I dropped from the swelling in my heart. As it was, I was admitted to an intensive care unit for several days.

All of my childhood, I had been taught to ask "What can I do to help?" but not "What can I do to be happy?" I was a painfully conscientious person inclined to take responsibility for everyone in my community. Never in my life had I used a phrase like "blow it off." If duty called, I saluted. I had not learned to set limits with others or to say no.

In Beaver City and Lincoln, I could manage with my particular personality and feel reasonably useful and happy. I could cope with demands and still find time to relax and enjoy myself. But with the success of *Reviving Ophelia*, my "way of being" was no longer possible. My inability to disappoint others or to disconnect from relationships was a recipe for disaster. I soon became a person who worked all the time and who felt responsible for more people than it was humanly possible to care for. My life entirely stopped being about me.

Success is a funny concept. People think they want it until they have it. Striving toward a goal is a great experience. Reaching it is often a different story. I learned many things from my life in the fast lane, and perhaps nothing more intensely than "Be careful what you wish for, you just might get it."

SECOND
LIFETIME

AVALANCHE OF ROSES
(1994–2002)

J ust after *Reviving Ophelia* was published, I gave my first radio
interview—twenty minutes on a local book show with my Unitarian minister. Two weeks later, Terry Gross interviewed me for
an hour for National Public Radio's *Fresh Air.* Shortly after that, I
appeared on *Oprah.* Soon, my publishing company was shipping
my book around the country in boxes stamped "Red Hot." When
I walked into a bookstore in Brookline, Massachusetts, the owner
gently guided me over to his wall of best-sellers. My book was number one. I was too stunned to speak. This simply could not be happening to me.

I cannot describe how unprepared I was for all of this. I felt as
if I had walked out my front door and into the path of a Boeing
727. Except for my self-published book *Hunger Pains,* I had no
knowledge of how book publishing worked. I knew nothing of
green rooms, publicists, radio tours or serial rights. I didn't own a
cell phone, and I had never stayed in a hotel with room service. I

didn't know how to hail a taxi, use a microphone or buzz myself into a building.

I had never been in a city on the East Coast or visited a newsroom, and was nervous about travel and crime. When I first visited New York to consult with my editor, I carried a decoy purse so that if someone snatched my big purse, my real one would still be close to my body and safe. That same trip, my seatmate on a city bus was an exhibitionist. I felt something touch my leg and looked down to see him masturbating. I jumped off the bus in a very sketchy part of the city. I had no idea where I was, and I suspect I would have been safer on the bus with the exhibitionist.

I journeyed from a life I understood into one that I didn't. I came up with the phrase "avalanched by roses" to describe what happened to me. I was deluged with offers to speak and requests for various kinds of help. I felt honored by all this attention, but I couldn't find the time to help everyone or even respond respectfully to every request. I felt completely overwhelmed. Roses, I realized, could cut off oxygen just as quickly as mud or snow.

I thought the uproar would be short-lived and that I would just tough things out for a year or two. I tried to continue all my previous activities while piling all the new ones on top. Until Jim and I closed our psychotherapy office in 2000, I continued to supervise psychology graduate students in their clinical training and work as a therapist. In that time, I also wrote two more books, *The Shelter of Each Other* and *Another Country*. I honestly don't know how I did it. I had no time for what Jim fondly referred to as "west and welaxation." I was as ragged as an old flag.

Shelby Foote wrote, "There is no more dangerous place on earth than right under the mouth of the horn of plenty." I can attest to his wisdom. During my early years of writing and speaking, I felt that all my important relationships were at risk.

Jim had not signed on to be the husband of a stressed-out writer. Since our marriage, Jim has been my Rock of Gibraltar. He is the personification of the word "solid," and, to use his highest words of praise, "a class act." He has many admirable qualities, but for me his most important quality is his staying power. He will never leave me. However, in my darkest hours, I worried that he might consider it. He grew tired of being Mary Pipher's husband at events and of spending his free time working as my booking agent and assistant. He missed a wife who had time for picnics, stargazing and concerts. He missed a wife who laughed.

My children had loved their happy, calm and nurturing mother. They hadn't volunteered for our new situation, and they didn't much like it. As young adults, they were moving out into the world and they needed a safe and familiar home base. They wanted an undistracted set of parents to notice their growth and victories, not overworked parents who were dashing around the country.

There is an old saw that fits my situation: "If everything is coming your way, you are in the wrong lane." I was extraordinarily lucky by the world's standards, but I was also out of step with the rest of the human race. I couldn't find a peer group. I didn't think anyone felt like me, and I no longer felt like other people. I didn't even feel like me.

My friends weren't quite sure what to make of me. Some were understandably jealous, while others simply commented that I was "different" or "not my old self." Mostly, though, they just missed me. And many of them wished I were having more fun with my good fortune.

By now I have met many people who make their living the way
I do. Many of us feel a strong sense of mission with our work, and
travel more than is pleasurable or sensible. When I've shared my
stressed reactions with other speakers, many of them have confessed
to the same kinds of experiences and breakdowns. One psychologist
friend abandoned his speaking career because it was, in his words,
"too brutal." Another described a day in which she had given three
speeches in three cities. She said ruefully, "I did a good job at each
one, but that night it took me five hours to go to sleep."

During their years of success, some speakers became addicted to
drugs or alcohol. Others developed health problems such as stomach ailments, hypertension and heart arrhythmias. Several writers
I know became estranged from their long-term partners, friends or
children. Every one of them reported recurring work-related
nightmares. While many politicians and a few speakers seemed to
thrive on attention, most writers I've met were wired as I am. The
fault was not so much our psyches but our circumstances.

The outcome of success is a well-known cultural story. Saint
Teresa of Ávila referred to this when she said, "Answered prayers
cause more tears than those that remain unanswered." The year
of photographer Ansel Adams's greatest success was also his year of
greatest despair. He had a show at Alfred Stieglitz's Gallery 291 in
New York, but also suffered a nervous breakdown and required
hospitalization. After *On the Road* became a smashing success, Jack
Kerouac moved back home with his mother and drank his life
away. In *Born Standing Up: A Comic's Life*, Steve Martin wrote of
the panic attacks and depression that came with his popularity.
The tragic lives of Sam Cooke, Howard Hughes, Janis Joplin and
Kurt Cobain exemplify the corrosive power of fame.

I can't imagine how wildly successful movie stars, especially the young ones, are able to handle their lives. After all, when I moved into the limelight, I was forty-seven years old with a family, a career and a community. Compared with a Matt Damon or Angelina Jolie, I am a small potato. When the traumas of Britney Spears, Lindsay Lohan or anyone else make headlines, I don't laugh at the public mocking. Rather, I feel empathy and sorrow. I have a sense for how miserable these celebrities must be.

After Malcolm Lowry published his best-selling novel, *Under the Volcano*, he led a desolate and unproductive life. In a letter, he wrote, "Success may well be the worst possible thing that could happen to any serious author." When members of the Band were asked why they were getting off the road, they responded simply, "This stuff can kill you." The road almost did kill Norman Cousins, who wrote in *The Healing Heart* about his near-fatal heart attack, which he attributed to his life as a traveling speaker. From book-tour escorts, I've heard about the mountain climbers, pro-football players and criminal attorneys who, for health and mental health reasons, ditched their tours midway and returned home.

My trauma around success was not uncommon, but I had my own way of falling apart. The expectations I carried from my childhood were a heavy burden. My mother required herself to be unfailingly kind and competent with all the people she served. Mistakes were not tolerated. No matter how tired she was, she would wake when the phone rang, quickly dress and dash out the door to be of service. If she spent the night with a dying patient, she would gulp down strong coffee and proceed cheerfully to her office for a fifteen-hour day. Her personal needs were irrelevant. I expected no less of myself.

I grew up believing that unless I was in acute pain or near death's door, complaining was immoral. In comparison with the hardships of 99.99 percent of the human race, my own suffering was trivial. I thought it was my duty not only to be cheerful but to feel cheerful. I thought that my troubles were mine to deal with and that my negative feelings indicated character flaws. This tendency to bury all pain and discomfort caused me trouble on the road. As my body increasingly told me I was in too deep, my brain continually ordered me to ignore that message and perk up.

My father's angry outbursts left me with a dread of hot-tempered men. Mr. Swift, the coach and swim teacher in Beaver City, left me feeling pretty helpless around bullies. As a therapist and teacher, I could be assertive when I had to be, but I preferred a gentle approach. My core response to conflict was to avoid it. On the road, this left me both emotionally unprepared and verbally unskilled to deal with hostile questions or argumentative radio hosts. When an aggressive audience member attacked my ideas, I wanted to flee. While carefully responding to confrontation, I'd stew in my own adrenaline.

Publishing has been my ultimate "both/and experience." It was both glorious and horrific. Almost as soon as I met Success, I met her evil twin, Pressure. I've benefited in a hundred ways from my good fortune. Yet it introduced so much density into my life that it almost sank my small boat of self.

My public life was both an honor and a great responsibility. I felt privileged to have a voice in a country where most people are voiceless. It was deeply touching to me that people cared about my ideas about issues. When I traveled and spoke, especially in rural areas and in the Midwest, women who reminded me of my aunts would approach me and say, "You say just what I would say if anybody was listening to me."

I felt grateful when I could be useful. Letters from adolescent

girls, mothers, older people or refugees gave me joy. I liked reading about girls' empowerment clubs, family co-ops, coming-of-age
ceremonies or intergenerational bonding programs. I felt honored
to meet with students who worked for refugees, with writing
groups or with therapists who appreciated my ideas.

But I was also crushed by my sense of responsibility. I wanted
my readers to benefit from my books, my publishers to sell the
copies they had printed and radio interviewers to feel satisfied
with my discussions. At speeches, I hoped the organizers and the
funders would be pleased with my work and that people in the audience would have their needs met. I wanted the participants to
feel that their questions were answered, the booksellers to sell their
wares and everyone in the book line to feel nurtured and respected.
When I couldn't make all of this happen, my conscience would
pummel me.

Even during my most stressful years, I never stopped loving to
write. When I was home, I spent my mornings in my study im-
mersed in a challenging yet sustaining process. I learned to think
on paper, to go deeper into my ideas and to find that quiet place in
myself that allowed the muse to come knocking. There was nothing in the world that made me feel luckier than that I was able to
make a living as a writer.

Vacation travel and work travel are as related as, to quote Mark
Twain, lightning and lightning bugs. One year I slept in hotel
rooms more nights than I did in my own bed. I came to dread the
phones I couldn't work, the car alarms on the street outside and
the heating and air-conditioning systems that either didn't func-
tion or sounded like lawn mowers. I endured my share of tepid
baths and showers and slept in too many rooms whose windows
overlooked a wall or a dumpster.

One afternoon, in Washington, D.C., on my way to my hotel room after a morning of interviews, the elevator stalled between the twelfth and fourteenth floors. I was stuck alone for almost five hours before repairmen were able to free me. Another time at an event in Georgia, a man on a call-in radio show threatened to do me physical harm. The event organizers played the tape of this interaction to the FBI, and they sent an armed agent to escort me from place to place. Once, in Detroit, the woman who drove me to my hotel after a speech had clearly snorted cocaine and was all hopped up. I wanted to jump out of her car, but it was below zero, late at night and I had no cell phone.

Yet I also learned how beautiful our country is. I have been able to work in Denali National Park in Alaska and at a school near Diamond Head in Hawaii. When I worked in New Hampshire, I stayed in a cabin on Squam Lake, where *On Golden Pond* was filmed. On day trips after events, I have hiked in Acadia, the Cascades, the Rockies and Sabino Canyon. I've touched the bristle cone pines of Colorado, the live oaks of South Carolina, the redwoods of the Oregon coast and the saguaros of the Southwest. I've strolled around Charleston, Boston, Washington, D.C., and Austin. I've been able to travel to and work in Poland, Puerto Rico, South Africa and much of Canada.

My favorite experience was a series of workshops for the U.S. Army and the International Girl Scouts in Tokyo and Okinawa. I spoke about sex roles and gender issues. My father had served in both places during World War Two. He had been a "grunt," living in a tent or in barracks. I was given general's quarters and a vacation house on the South China Sea. As I looked out on the ocean or walked the grounds of Camp Zama in Tokyo, I thought a great deal about my father. As I stood before the troops, many of them also poor kids from the South, I told them about my father's years in the service. My dad would have liked that.

I heard many war stories in Okinawa from local residents. When I visited the turtle-shell graves built into mountains, or the cliffs that local people jumped from to avoid being captured by the invading American troops, I felt connected to my father, who most likely stood in the same places. As Jim and I hiked through a rain forest, I realized my father had carried a stretcher and dodged bullets in this same mountainous area that we were enjoying.

No matter where I traveled as a speaker, people shared meals with me and gave me the gift of their life stories. When I spoke at a Catholic school in St. Louis, I stayed in a residence hall of the nuns. I awoke to the sound of women singing matins. I spent an evening with inner-city girls in Detroit. I was able to meet Fred Rogers, Katie Couric and Hillary Clinton, as well as mental health professionals doing community work, heads of schools, hospitals and nonprofits, leaders of family camps and co-housing projects. Every place I visited, I talked to people whose suffering, quiet courage and decency touched my heart. I was able to spend my days in a continuing education program on the human race.

At the same time, in the company of strangers, I felt alone, a familiar and traumatic experience for me. My life has been a quest to feel *felt*. Since I was young, I have looked for kind and careful attention. During my years as an adult, I've lived in the same place surrounded by family and various tribes of loyal friends. I chose a profession, psychotherapy, that allowed me to stay connected and authentic. I was deeply touched by people I met as a speaker. I even felt love for them. But in my interactions with them, I did not feel real to myself.

Being on the road somehow tapped into my childhood reactions to loss and loneliness. These weren't stored with language, but rather with physiological reactions, images and sensations. Events I didn't even notice on a conscious level could trigger inexplicable anxiety and despair. I would feel what I call "squishy," a physiological state in which I am shaky, light-headed and dizzy. When I am squishy, I feel fragile, empty and surrounded by darkness. During my adult years in Nebraska, I had rarely felt this way, but far from home, I experienced that feeling all the time.

In hotel rooms when I tried to fall asleep, my body would rev up. I was wired-tired with an arousal system on overload. I'd break into a cold sweat and feel my heart turning like a small, trapped animal in my chest. My self-talk would be rational and positive, but my limbic system was shouting, "Danger, warning!"

My overwrought nervous system sped up my thoughts. I would worry about my event the next day, my children having car wrecks, the extinction of our local Salt Creek beetle and whether I'd turned off my coffeepot at home. I would feel the way I had in the second grade and was alone in the hospital room awaiting my appendectomy. I was goofy and wild-eyed with fear. If a doctor had been in the room, I would have bit him.

Over time I became more, not less, self-conscious. Rather than habituate to public life, I became more traumatized by it. Crowds and travel left me feeling jittery and scattered, and before I had time to repair myself, I'd be back on the road. Even when I was home, I couldn't settle down. I rushed about in a state of emotional vertigo. My books and my walks couldn't always soothe me.

I began having conditioned stress responses to almost everything involving speeches. I could tell myself that I had given a certain speech many times and that I was unlikely to suffer much at the hands of Methodist ministers or California psychologists.

However, all kinds of small sensory cues triggered alarm bells. Many of these reactions didn't even reach a conscious level, but my body would tense up.

On the road, I lost my appetite and, in fact, became nauseated in airports and other frenetic places. I experienced the hot and cold flashes, the heart palpitations and the short attention span of a highly stressed person. If I heard a sudden loud sound, I would jump as if I had been electroshocked. At first I was confused by this intensifying anxiety. I had predicted I would become accustomed to my new career. Later, though, I met other speakers who had experienced the same phenomenon: The longer they were on the road, the harder it became.

Over the years, I developed more and more anxiety dreams. I dreamed of missing airplanes, of losing my notes and of not knowing what city I was in or how to return to Lincoln. I often dreamed that, unbeknownst to me, I was the only one naked in a room full of people. After I left the room, I would see myself in a mirror and feel humiliated. My most common dream was that I was surrounded by dozens of people's hands and arms—all grabbing at me. I couldn't see the people, only all those hands pulling at my clothes and body.

My extreme and uncharacteristic reactions to events frightened me. Once in O'Hare Airport on a snowy Saturday, I needed to catch my connecting flight home or I would be stranded at an airport hotel all weekend. My daughter was giving a speech in Lincoln that afternoon and I had promised to attend. For three days, I had been away from home, working in a hotel conference center encircled by highways, with no swimming pool or places to walk. I raced through O'Hare, but just as I arrived at my gate, the attendant closed the door to the jetway and refused to open it. I fell to

the floor of the terminal sobbing, something so utterly uncharacteristic of me as to be deeply unnerving. Even as I made a scene, I
asked myself, "Who is this crazy woman in my body?"

In Brown County, Indiana, I presented daylong workshops to
mental health professionals two days in a row. The night before
the first workshop, I lay awake all night alternating between shiv-
ering with cold and sweating profusely. No doubt I was pouring
battery acid into my brain with all those stress hormones. The next
morning, I drank a pot of coffee and somehow powered through
the day. I told myself I would be so exhausted I would surely sleep
the next night. Instead, I endured another night of jumping out of
my skin. By the following morning, when I faced four hundred
people for another day, I could barely hold my thoughts together.
I almost fainted several times during the workshop. To this day, I
don't know how I managed to make it through that experience.

By 2002, I found myself in the oddest spot imaginable. My career was going well, I had good and useful work—and I was absolutely miserable. There was a widening divide between how others
viewed me and how I viewed myself. People thought I was lucky
and happy, when in fact I was sadder and lonelier than I had been
in decades. I had stopped feeling like an energetic, maturing person, and I didn't recognize or want to be the person I had become.
All my life I had put mind over matter and I expected I could continue doing that, but my body was shouting at me, "No, you can't!"

Years earlier I had read William Styron's *Darkness Visible*, in
which he described the panic and depression that overcame him at
the height of his success. He developed relentless and untreatable
insomnia and recalled his mental state as "a veritable howling
tempest in the brain." I too felt as if my mind was infected. I felt
an odd combination of being totally naked and utterly hidden.

I had always prided myself on being an authentic person whose behavior and values were in accord with her thoughts and words. Now I felt as if I were acting like my old self, but inside I was very changed. I wasn't leading a real life; rather, I was lost in a shadowy dream. The more acclaim I experienced, the more I shrank inside. By the time I had my meltdown, I had almost disappeared.

RECOVERY

(2002–2003)

For a decade I had roared through a life of adrenaline surges and constant pressure to achieve more, better and faster. Only a train wreck could slow me down. Sitting in a lousy café on a drizzly day and thinking I was tasting fecal matter in my chili, my train crashed. I realized I could no longer live the life I was leading. I wasn't sure I even wanted to live at all, because no matter where I was, my mind was on full throttle. As Raymond Carver put it, "I was too nervous to eat pie."

That day I wanted only to be left alone. I no longer had the capacity to enjoy anything. I looked at the world through shitmucklety-colored glasses. I had stopped laughing. I had no energy or ability to carry on.

Thoreau suggested in *On Walden Pond* that the first step toward self-reclamation was to simplify, simplify, simplify. So that is what I did. I was fortunate my work schedule was flexible enough to allow me to do this. Over the years, I have had many friends, family members and therapy clients who could have greatly benefited

from a resting cure. I wish more depressed and weary people could
grant themselves vacations from ordinary life.

My initial act was to construct a gentler schedule for myself.
Mornings, I continued to write—I was working on *Letters to a
Young Therapist*—but otherwise I declared myself off the clock.
Jim and I made some intentional decisions about time. We called
a permanent halt on daylong workshops and extended book tours.

I greatly reduced the amount of information I recieved from
the outside world. While I had never watched television, now I cut
back on listening to the radio as well as reading the newspaper and
magazines. That winter, I declared a moratorium on reading books
about genocide, global climate change and the war in the Middle
East. Instead, I read Elinor Lipman novels and Sue Grafton mys-
teries. Until I dialed down my news intake, I hadn't realized how
onerous 24/7 updates on the world had been.

Also, I limited my encounters with people. I gave myself permission to skip holiday gatherings and to postpone social obliga-
tions. I erased calendar engagements until I had three months of
"white space" in my future. For the first time in years, I could
wake up in the morning and ask myself what I felt like doing.
Generally, my answer was, "Absolutely nothing."

Since I had worked most of my adult life with depressed people,
I understood intellectually a great deal about treating depression.
Still, I was of little help to myself. I was a resistant, argumentative
client. Even focusing all of my analytical skills and best advice on
myself, I didn't cheer up. Alas, I was learning that my head could
not solve the problems of my head.

I asked my doctor for antidepressants. I had never expected I
would do that. As a therapist, I recommended medication only
when every other solution had been tried and found to be inade-

quate. Though that winter I was resting, reading and exercising, I could not quiet my mind enough to sleep. So I gave myself permission to do what I had encouraged some of my depressed clients to do. Why should I hold myself to a different standard?

After only a few weeks on medicine, I felt a little less frantic. My overheated mind slowed down and I was able to deal with my punishing thoughts. My black moods still enveloped me, but less frequently. Best of all, I could sleep. Just being rested for the first time in years made me feel optimistic. I had some energy to make some positive changes in my life.

I made another important decision: I was finished with the self-improvement projects I had launched my whole life. All of my goals to better myself had become gaols, prisons that kept me from accepting myself. My constant efforts to improve had been a form of self-aggression. Now I wanted to accept myself as I was. Psychologist Carl Rogers formulated what he called "the paradox of change," which is that people can change only in an environment of utter acceptance and regard. I wanted to create a mental environment in which I viewed myself as someone who deserved to be understood and cherished, rather than criticized and improved. My goal was healing and self-reclamation.

I spent hours petting my old Siamese cat, Woody. I bought myself fresh flowers and herbal teas. I made *pozole* and chicken curry. To cool down my agitated brain, I played solitaire and listened to classical music. Dressed in sweat pants, T-shirts and thick warm socks, I watched the snowfall and the winter birds.

As weeks passed with this regimen of seclusion and self-care, I felt a small sense of relief. I was doing what my body and spirit wanted me to do. I had arrested the process of depletion, and slowly, very slowly, I was replenishing myself. I had always been a person who lived in my head and who viewed my body as a container for my busy mind. Now I had no choice but to pay attention to my body. My muscles were sore from stress. My heart raced and skipped beats. My adrenaline system was pumping toxic chemicals into my system. I was as stricken with remorse and wound up as a trauma victim. The long-neglected territory of my body called out for kindness.

For the first time in my life, I signed up for a yoga class at a nearby church. I approached my first session fearfully. I felt self-conscious about my body, and I was sure that I couldn't do the exercises. I experienced the same kind of anxiety approaching yoga as I had on the playground in elementary school.

However, yoga class was the opposite of the schoolyard in Beaver City. Quiet, gentle women welcomed me into a peaceful, high-ceilinged room. A wonderful teacher named Margaret reassured me that whatever I did would be fine. Slowly and carefully, she guided our group through relaxing movements. Thanks to her, I learned to notice where I was tense. She taught me to stretch and loosen muscles and to attend to my breathing and my posture, and she helped me make connections between a relaxed body and a relaxed mind.

My friends encouraged me to try massage. Even though I had been offered free massages when I taught at the Omega Institute, I had always refused them. I didn't like the idea of a stranger touching my body. I was embarrassed at the thought of taking off my clothes. For a flower child from Berkeley, I was pretty modest. Now, though, I was ready to give massage a try. I scheduled an appointment with a woman known for her kindness and skill.

When Heidi asked me where I felt sore, I answered, "I don't know. Everywhere."

First she rubbed my shoulders and upper back. I felt knots of pain everywhere she touched. I had no idea how much tightness I carried until I felt it slipping away. By the time I left an hour later, I felt wonderful, both physically and mentally. I had learned two things—how tense I could be and how relaxed I could be. I couldn't believe I had waited more than fifty years for my first massage. How I wished I had known its benefits earlier so that I could have prescribed it for my clients.

Yoga and massage helped me see that instead of ignoring my body's signals, I could grant them authority to teach me about myself. I looked for opportunities to learn more about my body. I listened to it. I noticed the tension in my neck after a morning's writing. I noticed the way my muscles softened and warmed when I swam. These were wonderful lessons for me.

In *The Boy Who Was Raised as a Dog*, authors Bruce Perry and Maia Szalavitz describe their healing work with traumatized children. They operated at the most basic levels with these children. Three of their techniques were particularly striking to me. Because children who are traumatized while young often have balance and coordination problems, these doctors hired a music and dance teacher. As the children learned to be more rhythmic, their body rhythms settled down into more normal patterns and they lost their heart arrhythmias and other physical symptoms of early childhood trauma. They hired a massage therapist to give the children healing massages, and also a large, loving woman whose full-time job it was to hug, rock and snuggle the children. Under this regimen, most of the damaged children slowly healed.

As a therapist, I had worked with traumatized refugees to construct "healing packages" of activities, resources and comforts to help them to recover from their traumas. They would tell me what they needed to feel better, and I would consult with them about how to obtain it. We would find them practical things such as city parks, English classes, dentists and honest used-car dealers. Many refugees said the activities that would make them happiest were quiet time outdoors, finding a religious community, meals with people from their homelands and activities that made them laugh and enjoy life.

The essence of my personal healing package was to keep my life as simple and quiet as possible and to allow myself sensual comforts and small pleasures. These are ancient ways of calming troubled nerves. Many religions have retreat centers, and in the 1800s in Europe, both tuberculosis and insanity were treated by time in sanitariums for rest cures. I didn't move to the Magic Mountain, but I created a mini-retreat center in my own home.

Water seems to be a universal elixir. People in all times and places have found water calming to live by, look at, walk along, sit beside or swim in. As I recovered, I walked on Holmes Lake Dam, swam at the university's indoor pool and read *New Yorker* magazines in the bathtub every evening.

The laying on of hands is curative in almost all cultures. *Curanderos*, shamans and Native American healers all touched their patients. Ama, the famous "Hugging Mother" of India, tours the world encouraging people to be kind and patient. She speaks to enormous crowds, and afterward, thousands of people line up for hugs. She is a tiny woman who often stands all night in crowded arenas hugging one person after another. After their bear hugs from Ama, many people report being physically healed or spiritually transformed.

Another worldwide cure seems to be the tastes and smells of familiar foods, especially those that remind us of our childhoods and families. After the tragedy at Virginia Tech, I heard a minister interviewed on public radio tell of meeting with students to ask what the church community could do to help. The students requested home cooking. They said, "We don't want to try to deal with all this while eating dorm food." I have no doubt the cooks of Blacksburg, Virginia, prepared scalloped potatoes, green bean casseroles, lasagnas and pies, all foods that helped those students cope with the tragic events.

During the winter of my discontent, I cooked familiar foods. I fried up *jaternice*, sweetbreads and perch. I bought sardines and Limburger cheese. I baked cornbread and made pots of pinto beans with ham hocks. I prepared dolmas and sukiyaki, oyster stew and *bulgogi*. When I tasted these dishes, I tasted something richer than food; I tasted home. I tasted time.

Laughter and humor are universal tonics. As I grow older, I attend more and more funerals. Of course, there are tears, especially if the death was sudden and unexpected. However, often during the services, family members tell jokes and we congregants laugh heartily. Later, in church basements, as we eat our sandwiches and cookies, we share more stories. The laughter is as much a part of the healing as the weeping.

In December 2002, I wasn't laughing much at all. But over the winter, I regained my sense of humor. Jim was persistent with his joking, his funny accents, impersonations and witty asides. I couldn't help but respond. My comedic children and my old cat made me laugh, as did my friends. Refugees especially were experts at using humor to cope with tough situations and to cheer others up. As my sense of humor returned, I realized how much I had missed it. I asked myself, "When did it go away? How long have I lived my life as if everything were a matter of life and death?"

Sometimes life offers us a healing package right when we need it most. I will be forever grateful that my first grandchild, Kate, born in 2001, lived nearby. Jim and I could drive to visit her. When I was with Kate, I never put her down. While she slept, I rocked her and sang her the same raspy lullabies my mother had sung to me. Snuggling with her, walking with her outside and reading her Mother Goose—all these actions were wonderful therapy. Kate made me laugh and helped put my problems in perspective. Whatever else was happening in my life and the world, I had a grandchild I could hold and enjoy.

Good memories from the past are also a balm. Often when I was with depressed clients, I would ask them to talk to me about their happiest moments. Couples who were bitterly estranged often would smile and soften as they recalled their first date, their wedding day or their honeymoon. Despairing teenagers would lighten up if we talked about their summer vacations with their grandparents or the day they brought home their pet.

The day my aunt Grace died, she was sitting in an armchair reading a yellowed newspaper article about my father's rescue of the man drowning in the Finley. She also had Otis's picture beside her. She fell asleep after looking at these two items and never woke up. When my mother was suffering with her last illness, I could cheer her up by telling her the childhood stories of her ranch life that she once told to me. In my own troubled time, I turned to family photo albums and decades-old letters from my mother and aunts.

I unpacked my childhood teacup collection and displayed it near my computer desk. The collection consisted of a dozen cups

from Mexico and other places my family had visited. My grandmothers had given me a few of them. I had one cup from our trip
to Whittier, California, to see Margaret and Fred. I found some of
the plates and pots I had made with Mrs. Van Cleave and put them
on display, too. These objects reminded me of happy times and
people who loved me long ago.

It helps to realize we are not alone. One thing I like to do is send
my silent good wishes to people all over the world who have problems exactly like my own. Contexts may change, but emotions are
universal. We can always pray for the people who are feeling as we
are at any given moment. "I pray for all the people who are lacking in confidence." "I send a blessing to those who are frightened."
As I pray for others who suffered, I join an ancient and populous
demographic group. My heart softens and I can feel mercy for
us all.

We all have our little rituals. The winter of my crisis, I understood I needed to reconnect with the natural world every day. That
harsh winter, I walked many miles every week on the frozen prairie. I was able to generate a few endorphins, but more important,
I connected to a deeper, slower time.

I found great comfort in my familiar routines and rituals. In
December, I watched the Leonids. I sat quietly, appreciating the
peacefulness of snow falling. In January, tiny snowdrops peeped
out from under a duvet of snow. The yellow aconites blossomed in
February; then, in March, the daffodils and jonquils saluted me
from the mud. I followed the cycles of the moon and the turning
of constellations and witnessed sunrises and sunsets. I was reset-
ting my internal clock and synchronizing my rhythms with slower,
more ancient ones.

My work as a writer helped me recover. Working alone in my

study was both soothing and exhilarating. Like many writers, I experience writing as a form of alchemy that turns pain into insight. That winter, I was drafting *Letters to a Young Therapist*. In a world that seemed out of control, I took great pleasure in reflecting about the work I had done for thirty years.

Poetry has helped many people put life in perspective. The best poets somehow point us toward wisdom beyond words. Many of my parents' generation had learned poetry by heart. My mother and my aunt Margaret took great comfort in reciting old favorites. My high school English teacher insisted we memorize poetry. She said that some of her students who fought in World War Two later told her that poetry by Blake, Whitman and Wordsworth comforted them in their foxholes. The winter of 2002, I read my old standbys—Billy Collins, Robert Frost, Mary Oliver and Ted Kooser.

Long Nebraska winters are perfect for reading hefty biographies. The winter of my recovery, I read biographies of Abe Lincoln. Since I was a child, he has been my hero. To this day, I find he has no equal in terms of empathy and knowledge of the human race. As a schoolgirl, I memorized lines from his second inaugural address. As I have grown older, I've cherished many of his more folksy lines such as: "Most folks are about as happy as they make up their minds to be" and "It has been my experience that folks with few vices have very few virtues." He was a great teacher of empathy: "Whenever I hear anyone arguing for slavery, I feel a strong impulse to see it tried on him personally." Lincoln had a simple, clear morality. "When I do good, I feel good; when I do bad, I feel bad, and that is my religion."

When I was a girl, Lincoln was my hero and he still is. He had a life of great suffering, yet his character saved him. Lincoln some-

how transformed all that misery into wisdom and compassion, and
personified our human capacity for sublimation.

In my family, I found role models for coping with adversity.
My aunt Grace watched her husband of seventy years slip into se-
nility. She cared for him in their home as long as she could. She
moved into assisted living with him when she could no longer care
for him alone. After Uncle Otis died, Grace lived for a year without him. Through it all, she kept on doing things that gave her
pleasure. She planted flowers and radishes and raised songbirds.
She cooked for the family, watched National Geographic specials
and made quilts.

My aunt Margaret sat by her husband of sixty years as he slowly
slipped away. Still, she managed to have fun and stay interested in
the world. She told me her secret was to find three things to enjoy
every day. I tried to follow her advice and at least appreciate a letter from one of my siblings, a good Mexican meal or a beautiful
song Jim played on his guitar.

My cousin Roberta helped me keep my sorrow in perspective.
She lost her husband in January, and I visited her in March. Roberta is in her seventies, but she is as fit and lively as a teenager.
One morning, she and I walked along the little creek near her
house. For a while we sat on a bench and she talked about her loss.
She spoke of her sorrow and loneliness, but she somehow didn't let
her grief define her.

Soon we set to work. We gathered the lime-green watercress
that flourished year-round at the mouths of springs. People in the
Ozarks once called it "winter greens," and before refrigerators and
shipped fruit, they ate it to prevent scurvy. Roberta and I pulled
cress from the small stream, twisted off the roots and tossed them

back in the spring. The roots would soon sprout new fresh greens. We stuffed our treasure into plastic bags. I carried most of it back to Nebraska with me, and for a week I could taste the Ozarks.

The person who most helped me through my depression was Jim. Before we headed into an event, he assured me I would be okay. He would hug me and quote Sergeant Phil Esterhaus from *Hill Street Blues,* "Let's be careful out there." We had our arguments and struggles, but he stayed by my side. As I read, he sat nearby working on crossword puzzles or strumming his guitar. We played Scrabble and watched movies starring Albert Brooks, Steve Martin and Woody Allen. We listened to beautiful music. Over morning coffee, we talked about our day. He helped me see that I had choices and that it was okay for me to say no.

Jim protected me in a hundred ways until I could again care for myself. He answered the phone, gave me foot rubs and accompanied me when I gave speeches. When we were far from home, he found parks and rivers for us to enjoy. He spotted the rare birds, the hill ablaze with azaleas, and the small perfect bookstore. When we sat for hours in the Chicago airport, he read beside me or found a quiet place for us to drink a cup of tea. Mainly though—and it is impossible to state how important this was for me—he was simply there. I trusted that no matter what came next, I would not be alone.

Years earlier, when *Reviving Ophelia* sold and my life began to change, I had a recurring dream in which I was being washed down a rapidly moving river. I couldn't catch hold of anything that would allow me to pull myself to shore. I washed past cottonwoods and picnic tables, and other friends on the shore who were desperately trying to save me. Then just as I gasped my last breaths,

Jim's arms reached out and hauled me onto the muddy warm bank. That winter I felt his arms pulling me back toward the shore, saving me from a different kind of drowning.

With March, the ice melted on the lake and the color green returned. After taking good care of my body for several months, it began to take good care of me. My blood pressure improved and my heart problems disappeared. After a few months of my simple, relatively stress-free life and my healing package of activities, I felt my depression lifting. I enjoyed the return of positive emotions: contentment, joy, calmness and new sparks of curiosity and energy. I again felt a great tenderness toward others.

By spring, I no longer felt so broken. I could breathe deeply for the first time in years. As I watched the songbirds return and the lilacs and forsythia burst into bloom, I felt as if I had survived a near-death experience. I thanked every tulip for blooming and every friend who called me for a walk.

I became more spontaneous. My friend Marni told me, "I never plan a day for myself as great as the one God has planned." She left blanks in her to-do list to see what happened in the white spaces. I followed her example and was delighted by what I experienced when I slowed down and let my days unfurl.

One afternoon, Jim, Sara and I were discussing the news of the day. Sara was working long hours at a difficult job that she was contemplating quitting. Jim's mother was in the hospital, and his father had prostate cancer. The world news was dreadful. We were all feeling whipped by the day, and no one had the energy to cheer up the group. As we glumly complained to each other, I changed the subject to hypotheticals. Who would we most like to dine with living or dead? We tossed out the names of family heroes—Nelson

Mandela, Eleanor Roosevelt, Benjamin Franklin, the Dalai Lama, Aung San Suu Kyi, Louis Armstrong, Jesus, Gandhi and Einstein.

Sara turned toward a discussion of our favorite meals, a popular topic in our family for generations. Soon we had brainstormed a menu for a perfect dinner: beef stroganoff, fresh raspberries and peach pie. Jim suggested we go buy the proper foods and fix that fantasy meal. Normally I would balk at a suggestion like that. I would protest, "I already have a meal planned for tonight," or "I need to use up the pesto." But that night, I agreed. We all shopped, cooked and feasted on our dream meal. By evening's end, we were laughing and enjoying each other once again. A day that just hours before Jim had labeled "a shit sandwich" became a bright memory.

If we live long enough, we will all experience times in which we feel lost in a deep forest. The first rule of the wilderness is "Don't panic." This may well be the first rule for life crises. What helped me and what seems to help others is slowing down, breathing, and simply being kind to one's animal body. Tincture of time and the reduction of stimulation heal troubled minds and overworked adrenaline systems. The most critical step is to stop banging ourselves in the head. We won't stop hurting ourselves until we lay down the hammers.

We all have within us the capacity not only to heal from crises but also to turn our sorrow into something new and strong. In fact, true growth requires spending time outside of one's comfort zone. Happiness need not be analyzed. Comfortable people tend to cling to their old patterns. Indeed, adults who have never suffered are shallow and, well, insufferable. Because they haven't experienced much pain, they haven't felt motivated to truly explore themselves and their relationships to the world.

We all suffer, but we don't all grow. Some people are so crippled by great sorrow that they die inside. Like a tree hit by lightning, they never recover. Some refugees are this way. Even after they escape the horrors of their home countries, they live shadow lives, going through the motions but never reconnecting with any life force that allows them joy and relationships. I know a Sudanese man who lost all of his family in that country's civil war. William's body is here with us, but his spirit died with his wife and children when a faraway village was burned to the ground.

Another man I know lost his wife twelve years ago. Since then, he has felt no interest in the world. He rarely showers or shaves and doesn't keep his home clean or see his friends. He says quite clearly that all of the meaning left his life when his wife died. Now this man is simply marking time until he can join his beloved. Fortunately, there are not many people who cannot heal from trauma. I am still hopeful that something good will happen to this sad man that will allow him to rejoin the living.

With crises, some people dig deeper into their entrenched identities and hide in the pup tent of their old beliefs. Many people simply numb themselves with television or self-medicate with alcohol and drugs. Some people blame all their pain on others and never examine their own role in creating problems. Other sufferers shrink their worlds into something small and manageable but actually quite false. People with eating disorders are an example of this narrowing of scope. The questions of the day boil down to simply "Have I gained weight?"

For all people, regardless of the crisis, the cure is always growth. Looking back from the vantage point of five years, I understand that my winter of sorrow was a gift. As Parker Palmer said in an interview, "To move closer to God is to move closer to everything, both joy and sorrow, light and darkness." We may experience post-traumatic stress reactions, but we are beginning a process of post-traumatic growth syndrome. Darkness and loss signal to us more clearly than anything else that it is time to expand our point of view.

A BIGGER CONTAINER

(2003–2007)

In November 2003, my writers' group traveled to a state park near Lincoln. We rented a cabin, heated soup and built a fire. We waited until it was dark, and put on our heaviest coats and our warmest caps and mittens. Then we carried our blankets and sleeping bags outside to observe an astronomical and a spiritual event. In a field of frozen prairie grass, we lay down to watch for the total lunar eclipse and the Harmonic Concordance, a six-pointed astrologically significant configuration.

The eclipse was breathtaking and, because we were together on a winter's night, even more magical than usual. However, we could not find the Grand Sextile. As we shivered and rued the bitterly cold weather, we pointed out shapes to each other and made half-hearted guesses, but we knew somehow that we were not seeing it. Then suddenly, I discovered it. I hadn't found it earlier because I hadn't looked with a big enough point of view. The Harmonic Concordance encompassed the entire sky.

We were right in the middle of this tetrahedron of stars. Just as

I grasped its enormity, I felt something I have never experienced before or since. I felt a lifting of my heart into the sky, as if I had been somehow pulled up and included in a celestial event.

At first, I couldn't speak or breathe. When I could talk, I shared what I saw with the other women. We lay beneath it, dazed and speechless. We held hands and breathed deeply together. Someone began to cry.

Later, sitting around a fireplace with cups of cocoa, we discussed our experience. Other women spoke of an opening of their hearts and a joining with the sky. We were fascinated by the idea that we couldn't find the Harmonic Concordance because our ideas about where to look were based on our past star searches. Only when we shifted to the whole bowl of sky could we see it. This experience is not unlike my experience of God.

Religions are metaphorical systems that give us bigger containers in which to hold our lives. A spiritual life allows us to move beyond the ego into something more universal. Religious experience carries us outside of clock time into eternal time. We open ourselves into something more complete and beautiful. This bigger vista is perhaps the most magnificent aspect of a religious experience.

There is a sense in which Karl Marx was correct when he said that religion is the opiate of the people. However, he was wrong to scoff at this. Religion can give us skills for climbing up onto a ledge above our suffering and looking down at it with a kind and open mind. This helps us calm down and connect to all of the world's sufferers. Since the beginning of human time, we have yearned for peace in the face of death, loss, anger and fear. In fact, it is often trauma that turns us toward the sacred, and it is the sacred that saves us.

The Alcoholics Anonymous movement has long appreciated the need for spiritual help in fighting addictions. Carl Jung wrote Bill Wilson of AA about drinking as a low-level search for union with God. Jung pointed out that the Latin *spiritus* refers to both the highest religious experience and the most depraving poison. He offered the helpful formula *Spiritus contra spiritum*. In other words, it takes something larger than ourselves to fight something that feels larger than we are, whether that is a craving for drink or unremitting despair. Before Alcoholics Anonymous was founded, no one had any success treating addictions. Alcoholism, when defined as a spiritual malady, became treatable.

In a famous scene in the movie *Jaws*, the local sheriff is chumming for the great white shark, and it appears out of nowhere. The shark is larger than the crew had imagined possible and they are terrified. The sheriff says carefully, "We're going to need a bigger boat." That scene could be a metaphor for my beliefs about religion. Most of us have that moment when we see our personal Jaws and realize we need an expanded point of view and stronger coping skills.

In the late 1990s, I attended my first Buddhist lecture since my days at Berkeley. Here is what I wrote after that experience.

When I walked in the door after work, my daughter suggested we attend a talk by Gelek Rimpoche from Jewel Heart, a Tibetan Buddhist center in Ann Arbor, Michigan. That day I had done seven hours of therapy and taught a class at the university over my lunch hour. Before I could go to sleep that night, I needed to prepare to testify in court as an expert witness, and just thinking of going to court made me feel stressed and grumpy. It was a gorgeous September evening and I wanted to cook dinner and, if the light held, go for a walk. However, I felt guilty when I turned down any educational experience. So I grudgingly agreed.

Sara and I drove to campus and followed Buddhist monks into the student union. They were barefoot, dressed in red and yellow robes, with shaved heads and prayerful demeanors. We paid our admission and hurried past the display tables selling incense, pictures of Gelek Rimpoche, and prayer beads. We entered a classroom with about one hundred people and, in what turned out to be an important error of judgment, selected seats far from any exits.

Just as we sat down, the president of Jewel Heart rose and introduced the speaker. Gelek Rimpoche was a middle-aged man, seated in a kingly chair, flanked by kneeling monks. He tapped the microphone and spoke softly in Tibetan. Five minutes later, he stopped talking and one of the monks, whose face I couldn't see, roughly translated his words. I say roughly because the translator monk didn't have a microphone and spoke little English. Many of his sentences had no verbs or made no sense. In this setting, Gelek Rimpoche wasn't charismatic. Neither he nor the translator offered smiles, pauses or variations in tone. Much of what was said was vague, jerky and repetitive.

"To be freed from the cycle of rebirth, one must practice nonattachment to escape the cycle of rebirth. This is what the Buddha means when he says to practice nonattachment and you will be freed from the cycle of rebirth." Excuse me?

Meanwhile, the room's temperature was rising from our body heat. Gelek Rimpoche seemed a little under the weather. He coughed frequently, cleared his throat and looked at his watch. I suspected that he too would have preferred a brisk walk, although no doubt he was less attached to the idea than I was.

To pass the time, I wrote to-do lists and notes to Sara. I pondered where I had lost my new pair of black tennis shoes. I analyzed my husband's mood at dinner and looked at my watch seven hundred times. Woefully, I noticed we had roughly two and a half more hours of this lecture.

To be fair to myself, I was a non-Buddhist who had sat in stuffy buildings all day. To be fair to Gelek Rimpoche, nobody is that well spoken through a clumsy interpreter. To be fair to the interpreter, his English was better than my Tibetan. Undoubtedly, this teacher had seen much suffering in his lifetime and was a wise, scholarly man with many profound observations on the human condition. However, compassion for the teacher didn't make me more patient.

In fact, I reflected sadly, I was as non-Buddhist as one can be. I was restless, greedy for experiences, self-absorbed, controlling, time-conscious and filled with yearning. I have strong feelings about granola. I even have intense complicated feelings about granola. With chagrin I observed that I was meditating more about our distance from the exit than I was about escaping the cycle of rebirth.

While his interpreter explained that all existence is a myth, Gelek Rimpoche scanned the audience for sleepers. I quickly became aware of my fear of being caught napping. I was also worried I would be reprimanded for my lack of attention. I was wriggling like a first grader who needed a bathroom. I wasn't eager to escape this world of attachment and illusion. I only wanted to escape this auditorium.

I didn't want to insult this good man, disturb the more devout attendees or even to wake the sleepers. But, by then, I had toughed it out for an hour and a half. I pondered such spiritual questions as whether there would be meals on my flights to Reno and if Jim had

videotaped *The West Wing* for me. I meditated on all the calls I
hadn't answered and wondered if any of them involved exciting
news or interesting opportunities. I considered whether the moon
had risen yet and if the temperature outside was dropping. When
our interpreter asked us to meditate for a half-hour on our state of
non-being, my being made a break for the exit.

After this uninspiring foray into Buddhism, it was several years
before I returned. When I did look again at Buddhist practices, it
was because I was in pain. My relaxation tapes and positive self-
talk were not enough to calm me down. Psychology, which had
helped me through past crises, wasn't powerful enough medicine
this time.

I love and respect my own field of study, but the winter of my
meltdown, when I viewed my situation in psychological terms, I
felt damaged. When I read Buddhist texts, I felt compassion toward
myself and other people. I could view all my experiences as lessons
in waking up.

Indeed, what I first framed as a mental health crisis, depression,
I came to see as a spiritual one. I needed a larger frame of refer-
ence in which to understand my situation. In the winter of 2002–
2003, I began a spiritual journey that continues to this day.

I approached Buddhism the way I approach almost everything.
I read books about it. Even though, at first, I didn't understand
much of what I was reading, I found the writing soothing. Reading made me feel lighter and more positive. It somehow gentled
me toward myself. I intuitively responded to Buddhist ideas. They
helped me see the world and my place in it more clearly.

There are as many versions of Buddhism as there are of Islam
or Christianity. My own understanding of it is a hodgepodge of

ideas I found useful from various schools. I loved Buddhism for its teachings in interconnectedness, the basic goodness of all living beings and the rightness of the world as it is. The belief that our lives are the creations of our minds certainly fit my experience. My external circumstances were excellent—a good family, good health, a great job, an adequate income and a nice place to live. Yet I considered myself unfathomable, unlovable and unfixable. It was the way I thought and felt about my life that caused me unhappiness.

I was drawn to the idea that I could be free of suffering. I longed to stop feeling guilty, driven and panicky. Yet, from the start, I imbibed lessons that gave me much more than symptom relief. I developed perspective skills.

I was captivated by the concept of mindfulness, which is described as a bird whose wings are compassion and awareness. I realized that my tendency to avoid confronting unpleasant reality had to do with my lack of compassion for myself. I couldn't afford to look too closely at events or I might see my own imperfections. When I did that, I punished myself mercilessly. Then again, if I could learn to accept myself in all situations, I could afford to see clearly. I could learn to be honest and gentle.

I attended local retreats and workshops on Buddhism. When Wes Nisker, meditation teacher and author of *Crazy Wisdom*, lectured in Lincoln, he pointed out that meditation is readily available at no cost. It can be done anywhere, at any time, for a few seconds or for most of one's life. All you need is your breath. As he put it, "Your breath: Don't leave home without it."

Not all my teachers inspired me. One teacher seemed especially attracted to the prettiest student in the room, and another was too New Agey for me. Another was such an austere perfectionist that I knew immediately I would never be able to satisfy him with my posture and my bowing. He reminded me of my swim teacher, Coach Swift, and I moved away from him as fast as I could. Still, I am grateful to all the teachers for their lessons in meditation and Buddhist thought. Women teachers especially helped me feel more tenderness toward myself and encouraged me to transform my fear and judgment into acceptance and curiosity.

I experienced short, guided meditations at workshops. I am not sure what exactly I was told, but what I heard is approximately this—"Sit straight with your knees below your hips so that energy can flow properly through your body, relax your abdomen muscles, keep your eyes open but unfocused, and follow your breathing. When you are distracted, gently return to attending to your breathing." These instructions sound simple, but at first I found them almost impossible to follow. My back hurt and my limbs grew stiff. I had a runaway mind. What the Buddhists call "monkey mind" was, in my case, "King Kong mind." I was so flooded with thoughts that I wondered if meditating might drive me crazy.

Theoretically, I wanted to meditate, but I found actually doing it extraordinarily difficult. As a therapist, I knew that we all want progress, but we resist change. I was a vivid example of this maxim. Figuring out my taxes and going to the dentist were easier than meditating. Even as I told myself meditation was a top priority, I worked to avoid that forty-five minutes alone with my mind. Meditating was a truly difficult internal art. As Wes Nisker put it, "It is hand-to-hand combat without hands."

In February 2003, I started to meditate regularly in my study. I sat on my new *zafu* (pillow) and *zabuton* (mat). My altar was nearby and I could look out on white pines to the south. I set a timer and tried to observe my breathing. I began with five minutes a day, and over the next few months, I worked up to forty-five minutes a day.

I am a disciplined person and I do what I promise myself I will do. At first, time passed as slowly as it had when I lay on my little mat in preschool. My nose itched, my stomach rumbled, my nearby computer signaled a new e-mail had arrived and I wondered who had sent it. I constantly caught myself drifting into sundry irrelevant thought sequences. Then I felt guilty and refocused on my breathing for maybe two breaths. By then, I was again thinking about dinner, upcoming vacations, our finances, my recent phone calls, my exercise regimen, my ineptitude at meditating and my family history. I wanted a Kleenex, a drink of water, a warmer room, a more comfortable position and the time to pass more rapidly. I wanted, wanted, wanted. I had many days when I was sure that the timer had broken or that I had missed its ring. Still, I stayed seated until the timer sounded. That was the one thing I had under my control.

Pema Chödrön writes, "The antidote to misery is to stay present." When I was able to be present and see the world clearly and with compassion, I always felt joy. Yet, at first, meditation made me conscious of how infrequently I inhabited the present moment. I was mostly lost in my usual obsessions and ruminations. While I was hoping for a better moment, I missed the one I was in. I once read a bumper sticker that proclaimed: "Having a Good Time. Wish I Were Here." That could have been coined for me.

After a few weeks, meditation became easier. One breath at a time, I reinhabited my body and soul. I experienced some moments when I simply observed my body, emotions and thoughts. I would feel a quiet peace as I listened to my heartbeat or simply noticed the energy in my hands or around my eyes. I observed small things such as the temperature of various parts of my body, tightness in my jaw or a feeling of weariness. Sometimes I realized that I was crying.

With meditation I found a ledge above the waterfall of my thoughts. It was similar to what my son had earlier described as my "going meta," only now I learned to do this whenever I wished. I could construct a bigger boat for myself when I needed it. I could step outside what was happening and observe it with more love, curiosity and openness.

Most of my days, my mind was on automatic pilot. I was having thoughts, but "I" wasn't thinking—a new distinction for me. I realized that I didn't control my thoughts, any more than I controlled my stomach growling. My rambling, discursive thought was not a crime, any more than was sneezing or breathing.

I experienced new things such as an awareness of the textures of my heart. Sometimes it seemed encased by a hard shell, as if it were a dipped cone. Other days, it was as soft and warm as pudding. I noticed that my larynx vibrated when I focused on it. I observed the strong, hot power at the base of my spine. I learned that when I tried to have thoughts, my mind would slow down and that sometimes I would smile. Best of all, when I was calmest, I often experienced a pulsing blue light in my mind that felt pure and beautiful.

I had many meditation sessions in which I felt both joy and despair, and peacefulness and anxiety. I had moments when I disappeared into a connected golden universe, and others in which I raked myself over the coals and feared I would never be free. I would have weeks when I felt I had made no progress. Then I would have an experience of openness and compassion. I began to depend on meditation for emotional centering. My body responded to it at some level I didn't understand. I was beginning to trust something other than reason.

The main thing I learned about myself from my first months of meditation was that I was a chronic, inveterate worrier. When I was a girl, perhaps my hypervigilance and constant anxiety about the future had been functional, but now it was not. Indeed, what I most needed in my life was the skill of calming down.

Meditation helped me settle down about insomnia, my most intractable problem. I would lie in bed and observe myself. At first, I'd be slightly nervous about falling asleep. I'd tell myself intellectually that I'd be fine, that I had a manageable day the next day, and that I was calm and happy. However, my body would begin to rev up. I could feel physiological tension increasing. I'd clamp my jaw. My heart would begin to race. My thoughts would speed up and I would feel hopeless about sleep.

At bedtime, all my adult life, I had carefully structured my thoughts with questions like these—What did you do today you are proud of? What are you grateful for? Whom do you most appreciate in your life? What are the ten best sunsets you can remember? On nights when I was lucky, I would fall asleep answering these relaxing questions. Other nights, I would get up and read for a few more hours. However, by 2002, when I tried to sleep, I suffered deeply conditioned panic. In fact, the phrase "tried to sleep" says it all. People who sleep well don't "try" to sleep. Trying to sleep is like trying to have an orgasm, trying to be happy or concentrating on being spontaneous—it doesn't work that way.

For years I had ordered myself around, and fought, judged and punished myself for my failure to sleep. Now, for the first time, I did something different. I stopped trying. I decided simply to study myself as I lay in bed, to note my reactions to the situation, to note my judging of my reactions, and to simply observe the whole catastrophe.

Almost immediately I felt better. I was no longer failing to fall asleep. I was succeeding at observing a process. I could see all the paradoxes—hurry up and go to sleep, you must calm down, I order you to relax, you are a bad person for not doing what you are incapable of doing, stop thinking. I could almost feel amusement. Somehow just noting all the complexity and absurdity of this made me more accepting of myself. I'd ask myself, "How would I feel if a patient told me this? Would I see them as pathetic? Would I help them? How would I do it?" Often, thinking about this, I could fall asleep, but when I couldn't, I would simply observe myself and rest.

Many nights, what helped the most was simply saying blessings for all the people I loved. I would pray for my colleague with cancer, for my relatives with special problems or for my friends who were in tough times. I would fall asleep feeling useful.

Meditation also taught me the difference between being awake and being habit-bound. I wanted reminders that helped me stay present. I had neither temple bells nor anyone who would ring them for me, so I decided that the song of birds would call my attention to the present moment. Whenever I heard a bird, I tried to remember to stop, breathe and observe what was happening. Fortunately, I have many birds around me most of the time.

As I attended my bells, I was amazed by the many unplanned but wondrous events I experienced. Carl Jung wrote, "Whether called or not, God will be present." As I learned ways to access that ever-present God, sometimes I could actually taste the ripe nectarine or see the tender way my husband bent over his guitar. I could hear the love in my daughter's voice.

As the months passed, I witnessed other signs of progress. I continued to have plenty of internal weather, but I gained some skills for dealing with the storms. I remembered my friend Steve's words to live by: "You can't worry about everything." I developed a shaky faith that, with meditation, I could make my life workable again. One morning, as I cleaned the kitchen, I noticed myself humming.

Often while meditating, I posed a question or suggested an issue for contemplation. Sometimes this would lead to a moment of clarity. One day, for example, I needed to make a difficult decision, and two people I loved and trusted had given me exactly the opposite advice on how to proceed. I bounced between their positions, reacting more than deciding. I feared letting either of them down. I also berated myself for being wishy-washy and lacking courage. I emptied my mind and waited. My insight was simple but apt: "Do nothing now. Be patient. Allow yourself time to clarify your thoughts. Whatever you decide will be right for you."

I discovered what could be called the power of the turning. This happened when I stayed present in the moment and didn't panic. Sadly, I was dangerously inept at that. In a crisis, my imagination runs away with me before my mind engages.

Once, when I was giving a keynote speech in Memphis, I woke in the night to go to the bathroom and I turned the wrong way. I didn't immediately recognize my mistake, and when I tried to enter what I thought was the bathroom, I stumbled into suitcases. Groggily, I thought that Jim had dumped his suitcase in front of the bathroom door. I kicked it away, then I tripped over some shoes.

I felt angry with Jim for causing me to trip in the dark. Still confused, I pushed forward into clothes and an ironing board. I asked myself, "Why would Jim hang up his clothes in the bathroom?"

Something wasn't right, but I stubbornly persisted. Finally, I stopped and observed myself struggling. I snapped awake and realized I was seeking the toilet in the closet.

This ridiculous experience is not unlike our process of growth. We keep pushing and pushing to get someplace, and then we stop and notice where we are. This awareness allows us to change course. We can shift our path and at least orient toward the right door.

As a therapist, I often observed the power of a breakaway idea. Of course I experienced my share of plodding sessions with routine questions such as, "Did you do your therapy homework assignment?" "Has your son been following the house rules?" "Did you keep a food journal?" Yet every now and then in the middle of a rather humdrum session, I would find myself saying something like, "What your son most needs is for you to sit by his side. He cannot communicate with you right now, but he needs to feel your loving presence." Or I would just toss my notes and say to a client, "Today we are going to tell jokes and talk about what makes you laugh." These fresh actions opened the session up into something larger and more spacious.

Prayer connects us with that which is vast and eternal, and it connects us with each other. For example, some Buddhists pray to Kwan Yin, goddess of compassion, "May this suffering serve to awaken compassion." All religious traditions encourage prayer as a portal to a bigger container.

Prayer is vastly superior to worry. With worry, we are helpless; with prayer, we are interceding. When I hear sad news, I try to say a prayer for the victims. When I am troubled, I will say a prayer that asks for relief for myself and for all those who suffer as I do. "I pray for all other people who feel anxious and edgy at this moment." When I am concerned about my relatives or friends, I say a short prayer to myself—"May they be happy and free of suffering."

My altar keeps me aware of the sacred. When I look at it, I am reminded of my family and friends, the mountains, the sea and the prairie. In its small way, it covers all I know of time and place, of people and trees, feathers and rocks. On it I have mementos of myself as a young girl and my most recent favorite bits of beauty. It is the physical manifestation of all that matters in my life.

When I am home, I meditate and pray beside my altar. Here is what sits on it today—a green cotton cloth from Thailand, a small jade Kwan Yin, a bronze Buddha, a picture of Uncle Otis and Aunt Grace, three lucky buckeyes, two shark's teeth, a sand dollar, stones from various places, a pipestone turtle, a mourning dove feather, a bird woven of banana leaves from Hawaii, Jim's hospital armband from his birth, paper prayer flags, a petrified fish, a pinecone, an acorn, prairie grasses, fresh flowers, a starfish, a beaded necklace from my granddaughter, a place marker I made for my mother when I was a Brownie in Beaver City and a fortune from a cookie that says, "Put the universe inside you. Make it your own."

Harold Kushner wrote, "Our awareness of God starts where self-sufficiency ends." My misery forced me to reflect, which led me to slow down and take better care of myself. These actions propelled me to meditation, which fostered calmness and an appreciation of the moment. Being present led me to the heart of the heart of the universe. For the rest of my life, when I need that place, I'll know how to find it.

DESPAIR AND
SELF-ACCEPTANCE

D espair is the subjective state we experience when our inner and outer resources are insufficient to cope with the situation at hand. At core it involves a breakdown in our trust of ourselves and the universe. It is a 911 call from deep within, warning us that we must make changes if we are to survive psychically.

Of course, my understanding of despair is more than theoretical. Many of my family members have battled addictions and struggled with emotional disorders. Both my parents and my husband's parents died slow, painful deaths. I've worked for thirty years as a therapist, listening to people share their darkest and saddest stories and I have interviewed refugees about Kosovo, Sierra Leone and Afghanistan. I feel qualified to write about what humans do with despair. I think all of us are qualified.

While I can't compare myself to Job, my anguish has carried me to many dark and lonely places. My suffering helps me connect to others who are coping with much darker scenarios. As I write this today, a young teacher I know lies in a nearby hospital dying of cancer. Most likely, someone reading this has lost a child in Iraq or is married to a person with Alzheimer's. Other readers stagger under money and health worries. Some are fighting foreclosure, prejudice or uncaring employers, while others are holding on to their sanity for dear life. I am no Job, but the world is full of people suffering as he did. For many people, facing the day requires extraordinary courage and self-discipline.

Most of the time we humans keep our suffering to ourselves. We are polite people who don't want to inflict our burdens on others. We are proud people who don't want to be pitied. Some of the time we keep our despair from ourselves.

One of the saddest things about despair is our attempt to deny it. To move toward our pain requires us to buck a well-tuned system of defenses. We repress, somatize, rationalize and avoid our own despair. Too often we give our deepest pain orders to march off a cliff, forgetting that this pain is our psyche's way of encouraging us to take it easy and offer ourselves some compassion.

We may banish despair from our consciousness, but it doesn't disappear. The stress hormones keep on pumping. Tightness in our chest, tension in our shoulders and a feeling of heat on our faces—all of these are attempts by our bodies to urge us to pay attention. The body signals us constantly about our inner and outer situations. It is our personal GPS, and we ignore it at our peril.

Our biggest problems come from our cover-ups. While facing anguish is difficult, not facing it is even harder. Our daily headlines tell stories of deflected despair. The unemployed father is arrested for road rage. A bullied teenager shoots his classmates. Shame and humiliation have motivated many a terrorist. Bars and nightclubs are full of people who cannot face pain.

After a life of running from my own pain, I realized I couldn't do it any longer. Full of fear and uncertainty, I embarked on a journey of self-exploration. I wanted to stop inflicting pain on myself and, instead, find my strengths and my goodness. Especially at first, I trudged through a pretty hellish set of discoveries—that I was a mess, that I had glossed over my childhood suffering, and that I was emotionally tapped out with nothing left to give away.

I shouldn't have been surprised that when I first looked deeply into myself, I felt crummy. I knew from experience that therapy clients often feel worse before they feel better. In their beginning sessions, they discuss their traumas and they cry or rage. They flail at themselves or others for weakness. Only later do they begin to see positives and discover strengths. People who meditate often talk about feeling crazy or uniquely weird during their first sits. Many describe sobbing and falling apart as they face their fears and sorrows. The journey toward a more examined life nearly always begins with pain.

Certain parts of my past were "no-fly zones." I remembered only a few of the many times my father had been angry. When we lived in the trailer in the Ozarks, Dad lost control a few times when he was punishing me. He didn't injure me physically, but his fury scared me. I had an almost dreamlike memory of a night in Beaver City when he threw a skillet across the kitchen toward my mother. Aunt Margaret told me about an incident at a lake when my cousin forgot to put the plug in the boat and it filled with water. My father was so angry that my uncles had to stop him from physically injuring my cousin. I was there, but I don't remember that.

Even if I could recall certain events, I felt no emotions about them. I could describe what happened, but I described it as if I were reading from a dictionary. My head remembered, but my body felt dead. One treatment for chronic pain is to literally freeze nerve endings with liquid nitrogen. I felt as if I had frozen the nerve endings that connected me to memories of my deepest sorrows. "No pain for me, thank you."

As I meditated on my childhood, I re-experienced some of these sorrows. I would recall a traumatic event and my stomach would ache. My jaw would clench. My heart would feel hard and cold. Sometimes I would cry; other times I felt as if I were locked in a block of ice. Afterward, I would be dazed for a few hours.

Gradually, I became more clear-eyed about my parents. I didn't love them less, but I did acknowledge that their actions had enormous consequences on the lives of my siblings and myself. Since I viewed myself as accountable, I had to hold my parents to some standards as well. This realization was incredibly painful. When I considered the effects of my parents' choices, I felt a stab of separation and disconnection. My chest hurt and my breathing became ragged. Still, I stayed with these feelings. Over time, I learned I could be more realistic about my parents' failings and still love them.

My discomfort with anger has always been pronounced. I have never been able to watch violent movies or television, or to read about domestic violence or child abuse. Sometimes I feel other people's pain in ways I do not feel my own. In Sunday school I had learned "Love thy neighbor as thyself," yet I was never really taught to love myself.

As I meditated about my past, I realized that I was seething with anger and that it was all directed toward myself. I was responsible for everything and to blame for everything. Whatever happened in my world, internally or externally, was my fault. Repeatedly I had failed to keep everyone content, and for that I condemned myself. This hanging judge was so much a part of me that, like breathing, I didn't notice it until I slowed down and really paid attention. When I did, it alarmed me. I had always seen myself as loving and gentle. Who knew how filled with venom I had become?

I had made myself my own grand inquisitor. If I had a weird nightmare about a reptile or a house fire, I would tell myself it was because I was nutty. If I dropped an egg on the counter and broke it, I would tell myself I was clumsy and careless. Of course, I knew other people had nightmares or broke things from time to time. While I could exempt them from judgment, I could not absolve myself.

With practice, I became more mindful of the rules I had made for myself. For example, if I woke up in a sour and surly mood, I would give myself a hard time. I'd ask myself, "What is wrong with you?" As I learned to observe my thought sequences carefully, I had a realization so simple that it is embarrassing to share. I thought, "Who does wake up sunny every morning?" I gave myself permission to join my fellow humans who don't arise from their beds smiling.

When my father was deeply critical of someone, he said, "He's no damn good." I realized that, at core, that is what I believed about myself. I constantly questioned my own thoughts, feelings and behavior. My answer to the "why" questions was always either "I'm no damn good" or "I'm screwed up."

Perhaps my core belief about myself was that I was not worthy. My deepest pain came from not seeing my own goodness. I felt so damn broken. I didn't trust myself just to be who I was. I felt I deserved my misery, even that I caused it. I could not see all the love and joy that I held within myself.

These ideas stemmed from my early years with absent parents. At the time, I couldn't blame them for being gone because I needed to love them. So instead, I blamed myself. Somehow I deserved to be lonely. I told myself that what I didn't get, I didn't need. By becoming the universal donor, I relinquished my rights to have needs.

Most of my life, I could dish out compassion, but I couldn't take it. I was extremely embarrassed by gifts or compliments. When people offered to help me, I almost always said, "No, I can handle it." "Don't worry about me." "No, I don't need any presents." "I like the leftovers." "I'll wear the hand-me-downs." Or, "I'll sit in the back middle seat." In my emerging life, I yearned to find ways to both accept love from others and extend it to myself.

Over time, through meditation, I acquired some ability to acknowledge whatever was happening. Sometimes I could smile at my intensity. I would have a thought sequence like this: I am aware of how hard it is to break through my own denial system. I feel heavy and I have goose bumps. I want to believe I am flawless and that the world is made of spun sugar. I don't believe it, though. My heart is racing. My mouth is dry. I am filled with flaws too awful to admit. What are my flaws? What can I confess to? I am often fearful and wary. I don't trust others as much as I think I should. I think I know everything. I think I know nothing. I am clumsy with others. I don't appreciate every moment to its fullest.

I would accept all those thoughts and then say a prayer for everyone who could turn drinking a cup of cider into a metaphysical event. All my life I had been told that I thought too much. I now learned to pray for humans who think too much. All things considered, we weren't such a bad lot.

Meditation helped me stay with my own experience and not censor or censure upsetting information. Instead of being utterly entangled in my thoughts and feelings, I learned to note them without judging them. I would even wait to pounce on a thought so that I could label it. Nothing slowed my thinking down more rapidly than that. I am just stubborn that way.

I read of a Buddhist teacher who developed Alzheimer's. He had retired from teaching because his memory was unreliable, but he made one exception for a reunion of his former students. When he walked onto the stage, he forgot everything, even where he was and why. However, he was a skilled Buddhist and he simply began sharing his feelings with the crowd. He said, "I am anxious. I feel stupid. I feel scared and dumb. I am worried that I am wasting everyone's time. I am fearful. I am embarrassing myself." After a few minutes of this, he remembered his talk and proceeded without apology. The students were deeply moved, not only by his wise teachings, but also by how he handled his failings.

There is a Buddhist saying, "No resistance, no demons." I worked to stop resisting my pain. I tried to look at myself with more curiosity and less judgment. I invited all my thoughts to the table and welcomed them like long-awaited guests. As I watched them come and go, I could sometimes see beneath my layers of pain, my desperately self-protective ego and my habitual ways of viewing the world. Sometimes I felt connected to something light and spacious.

Of course, it wasn't always that way. Some days I never escaped the Mary that I had been all my life. I berated myself for not breathing properly or for not noticing a sensation in just the right way, whatever that meant. I wanted to connect with wisdom and instead found contempt for myself. I wanted to feel humility, but often I felt self-humiliation.

Recognizing the immensity of my self-judgment was progress. It was impossible to solve a problem that I didn't recognize existed.

I learned to count the number of times I criticized myself during my half-hour meditations. Sometimes the number was as high as a hundred. Still, I was counting, not just judging. I began to cut myself some slack. A Buddhist friend told me that he had outgrown the need to judge himself and that he had found peace in simply being kinder to himself. His simple statement gave me hope.

I conducted a simple psychological exercise. I drew a picture of myself. I looked worn and worried with waves of dark energy emanating from my forehead, but I had a smile on my face and wide curious eyes. Then I sketched another of my biggest problems. I showed myself carrying a heavy bag filled with guilt, shame, self-loathing and dread. I was so weighed down by this bag I could barely walk. Finally, I drew another of myself with my biggest problem solved. Birds had carried away my huge pack of sorrows, and I was dancing with abandon and joy.

Slowly, I learned how to lift my heavy burden off my shoulders. One morning, I noticed this thought sequence: I woke up feeling happy and physically relaxed. Within ten seconds, I began to feel guilty because I was enjoying lying in bed. I asked myself, "Am I lazy?" Then I felt guilty because I hadn't gotten out of bed. "Am I depressed?" I wondered. Then I felt guilty because I thought I should get up. I asked myself, "Am I driven?" Finally, I felt neurotic because I had so many thoughts and couldn't simply enjoy lying in bed. I asked myself, "Am I salvageable?"

When I castigated myself this way, I followed Thich Nhat Hahn's example and told myself, "Darling, I love you just the way you are." I realized I was simply committing the crime of being human. When I thought of something I was ashamed of, such as "I am mad at Jim," I would pray for all the wives who had ever felt mad at their husbands. When I felt irritated with myself for doing something stupid, I would say a prayer for all the other people on earth who had made a silly mistake. That would make me smile and lighten up.

Instead of dividing my actions into good and bad ones, I studied what behaviors caused what results. I paid more attention to karma, or the fact that actions have consequences. If I was focused and cautious, I did less harm. When I thought carefully before I spoke, my words had a better effect. If I allowed myself time to rest in the late afternoon, I would be more cheerful at dinner. When I could put aside my own neediness and be present for another person, she benefited from my attention.

Paradoxically, as I embraced my basic goodness, I could be more honest about my shortcomings. When I had treated myself harshly, I had needed to deny my very real flaws and mistakes to avoid my own self-judgments. As a hanging judge whose every transgression merited the death penalty, I couldn't afford to see the effects of my behavior on others. Now I could face facts. I could admit that I had spoken too quickly or been unreasonable. After all, don't all of us make these mistakes?

I developed mantras to help with self-acceptance. "I forgive myself for losing perspective, for being fearful, for being overconfident and for lacking confidence. I forgive myself for being ungrateful and for chiding myself for not feeling gratitude every moment of my day. I forgive myself for the thoughtless remark, the inattentive moment, the careless gesture and the undelivered gift." "Forgiven, forgiven, forgiven. I am forgiven."

Although with others, I was not a demanding person, I had sent myself a different quality of message. I developed new ways of

dealing with myself. The first time I noticed I had changed was
when I accidentally spilled tomato juice on our light gray rug. My
internal dialogue began with my habitual responses: "You are stupid, careless, clumsy and awful," but suddenly I asked myself,
"How mad would you be at a friend who did this?" I smiled and
told myself, "Accidents happen. Let yourself off the hook."

I practiced what the Dalai Lama calls "inner disarmament." Of
course, I still had judgments, but I tried to accept even my judgments without judgment. At a glacial pace, I moved beyond re-
pression and self-criticism to something more skillful. I discovered
the difference between recoiling from feelings and opening to
them. I trained myself to be more curious than fearful. Sometimes
I even felt compassion for myself as I struggled.

One day I meditated about my body in this way: Oh, what a
complex subject. I loved my body when I snuggled into my mother's chest and sucked my meals. I loved the pudgy little body that
took its first step and the lithe one that turned somersaults and
dove off the high board. I hated my body at recess when it tripped
me at skip-rope and slowed me down during games of Red Rover
and tag. But I liked it just fine when I chugged on my bicycle
down a soft, hot highway with my girlfriends, my legs pumping
strong and fast, or when I paddled through silky Ozark lakewater
to climb onto a sun-drenched, slivery dock.

As a young woman, I saw my body mostly as a source of sorrow
and shame. When other girls grew breasts and curvy hips, I hated
it. Flat Chest and Puffy Stomach, the year I was fourteen, you
nearly destroyed my life. Even in college, when my first boyfriend
told me I was beautiful, I didn't believe him. At Berkeley, one of
the birthplaces of the women's movement, I criticized my appear-

ance. In my crowd, the folksingers, poets and campus leaders paired off with my prettiest, most buxom girlfriends. I raged to myself—How dare these men lecture others about revolution, equality and the Age of Aquarius, and then choose the same petite, demure women their fathers would have chosen?

After I married, I felt more accepted by men. That I was married proved something. Marriage allowed me to put my body on probation—it was okay as long as it functioned respectably. I liked how this body gave me two children and kept me lively and healthy. In fact, now would be a good time to offer my body an apology for those many decades when I routinely mistreated her— with smoking, alcohol, pots of caffeine, not to mention chips, doughnuts, and an almost total lack of vegetables. Dear body, please forgive me.

Fortunately, with middle age, I granted my body amnesty. Nobody much noticed its shape anymore, not even me. It was well fed, exercised daily and taken to the doctor for regular visits. My questions were about cholesterol and bone mass. I didn't ask, "Am I pretty?" but rather, "Can I still ice-skate, cross-country ski and carry a backpack up a mountain?"

One day as I meditated in my study, I looked out at our snow-bent white pines, the lake beyond and, across the lake, the observatory and the spruce- and fir-covered park. As I admired the view, I realized that the dam was built in the early 1960s. Before that, this area was cornfield or pasture. I was in my teens when the lake was formed and the first trees were planted. Now I am almost twenty years older than everything in my sight lines. My body has lasted longer than the tough old trees, the muddy lake with its trout and pelicans, and even the forested hills of the park. This small amalgamation of chemicals and electricity, of current and light, of heart beating and lungs pumping, has survived blizzards, food poisonings, surgeries, the deaths of parents and grandparents, the fall of empires, and its own adrenaline floods and sleepless nights.

Today I give myself the pleasure of valuing my body. I love my liver-spotted hands, my stretch marks, my shaggy hair and the map of my face. I praise this body that has kept me on this planet in this place, available for learning, adventure and warmth. I love how my senses allow me to drink in the world. Body, I thank you for giving me life. I will never disrespect you again.

Over time I discovered ways to soften my judgments and deal with what happens next in a less reactive, more accepting way. Sometimes when I hear my inner critic, I smile and say, "Hello, old pal. Where have you been? Welcome home." I am more able to focus on my good intentions. I know I want to do the right thing. I aspire to be happy and good. I recognize that I am disciplined most of the time. I try to focus on my courage, not my fears. On my best days, I can see myself with the eyes of someone who loves me and wants me to be happy. This nurturing person has always been there, but I am better now at finding her.

For years, I had been living under the tyranny of "shoulds." Most of my "shoulds" were my own choices, but I was living as if they were orders. Now I try to wake up every day and ask myself, "What do you want to do today?" Most days I do the same work I always have done, but I do it with less sense of burden and obligation. This small shift makes a big difference. As my heart has softened toward myself, so it has also softened toward others. I am less judgmental. I feel more humble and more trusting that others can find their own way. I am learning to love people without working so hard to improve them. When I see them struggling with their own angst, I feel a great sense of "just like me." I leave them be.

I notice this most on my weekly walks with my daughter. She works full time, but on Saturday she and her dog, Lucy, come over and we tromp around the lake. Sara talks about her friends and her work life. In the old days, I would have jumped in with opinions, helpful suggestions and commentary. Now I listen. I remark on Lucy's joy as she mucks about in the duckweed. I reassure Sara that she knows what is best. Do I still offer her unsolicited advice? Now and again. After all, I am a mother and no transition is flawless, but even Sara will avow I am much improved.

My granddaughter Kate taught me a great deal about my nurturing self. I was capable of giving her nonjudgmental, empathic and constant love. I accepted her imperfections and forgave her mistakes. I asked myself, "If Kate is fine just as she is, why can't I be as well?" As I related to her, I developed a new model for a nurturing self.

For example, Kate had painted a small unicorn at a nearby pottery place. Sadly, it broke in the firing process. Jim repaired it as best he could, and we all gathered around Kate to support her when she saw her cracked unicorn. I watched as her parents lovingly comforted her. Later, when I complimented Jamie on her skillful way of comforting Kate, Jamie said, "It won't be her last broken unicorn." I replied, "She is too young to realize that broken things are beautiful." As I spoke, I realized these words could apply to all of us, even me.

I had another Eureka! moment after one of Kate's visits. As I meditated beside my altar, I began thinking of my brothers and of my sorrow that I couldn't protect them from the hard lives we had as children. Suddenly, I saw our living room in Beaver City. It was late in the day, but none of us had turned on a light. My brothers were playing on the floor with a toy train. I saw myself standing nearby and watching them. I was seven or eight, slender with long, tangled hair and sad blue eyes. I was hungry and I wanted my mother to come home. I was only a year older than Jake, whom I felt responsible to care for. I weighed less than sixty pounds, and I was just learning to jump rope. I didn't know what I was doing any more than my brothers did. I could see the young, frightened Mary who tried to hide all her pain and fears behind the illusions that she was competent, in control and immune from pain herself.

I was barely older than Kate. Would I expect her to take care of children, eat meals without parents and suffer days without conversations or hugs? Would I want her to be forced to rescue her siblings from an angry parent? Would I expect her to make sure Claire and A.B. made it to and from school and had food to eat? Would I want her to deform her spirit with so much denial, guilt and premature responsibility?

The little Mary in the dark room moved toward me. I took her into my arms and pulled her to my chest. I held her tightly and stroked her hair. I felt great tenderness toward her. I wanted to love and protect this young, scared child. I whispered, "There, there. You are going to be okay now. I love you. I'll take good care of you." I felt her tense body relax into mine and she began to cry. I began to cry. We were the same person, the little Mary and the meditating Mary. We wept as one. At first our tears expressed heartbreak; then they changed to what we call in our family "happy tears."

When I rose from my cushion and dried my eyes, I felt new and free, as if I had been released from prison. Something hard and broken in me had fallen away. I had invited myself to live in my own heart. I could love and protect myself as fiercely as I did Kate.

After that, I had less trouble granting myself permission to stop work when I was tired, to eat when I was hungry, and even to be a little grumpy now and then. I stopped expecting myself to be perfect, but I also stopped beating myself up for yearning to be perfect. I could cut myself slack both ways. I could laugh at my self-torment. I reassured myself with comforting lines I heard my son and daughter-in-law say to Kate.

As I told myself some of the messages that Kate received, I realized that I always had said those things to other people. I tried to give others respect, empathy, forgiveness and freedom to maneuver. I gave to others what I wanted from them. There is a Yiddish word, *kvell*, which means to be so happy in another's joy that one's own heart swells with pleasure. I was quite capable of that.

For Christmas, I bought a rather expensive music box for a six-year-old Sudanese girl named Mary. As I explained my reasoning for the purchase to Jim, I said, "She is a good girl, a hard worker, and she doesn't get much attention." I could have been describing myself at six. I knew that Mary would love having something so beautiful just for herself. It gave me great pleasure to give her the music box.

I showered small mercies on myself as well. I bought a hammock so that I could read under our sugar maple tree. I gave myself permission to throw away the expired yogurt or the five-day-old kung pao shrimp. When I dropped ice cubes in the water glasses of my guests, I took the time to put ice in my own glass as well. I allowed myself to simply rest when I was tired. On a lovely day, I knocked off early and worked in my garden, no matter how much work was piled on my desk. And when I did that, I didn't just tackle the weeds with great fervor; I paused to look at the flowers and pick raspberries.

I granted myself the right to have the same needs as others had for nurturance and respect. I accepted gifts of kindness. My women friends asked to hold a wedding shower for my daughter. In the past, I would have said no. I don't like to be a bother or the recipient of attention and favors. Now I was ready to say yes and to be grateful.

The wedding shower was an amazing event, with elegant Thai flower arrangements, goldfish in tall clear vases, handmade menus and trays of exotic sushi. The young chef was a friend of our family, and my friends' husbands served the food and wine. I sat surrounded by my friends reminiscing about Sara's childhood, our campouts and parties of long ago, our children's hardships and victories, and our long-held enjoyment of each other. I felt enfolded in acceptance and lavished with attention. I didn't run from that. Several times during the evening, I noticed that tears covered my cheeks. Happy tears.

One day after I swam at the university, I was relaxing in the sauna. I told myself to stay in the sauna for at least ten minutes, but after five minutes I wanted to leave. I wrestled with myself: Was it healthier to discipline myself to stay ten minutes, or to simply do what I felt like doing? I wanted to do the right thing, and as is often the case, I couldn't figure out what it was. Finally, I just laughed at myself for my constant moral questioning. I realized that I didn't have to *be* good, I *was* good.

This epiphany was similar to the feeling I sometimes have when I look all over the house for my eyeglasses, only to realize I am wearing them. They have been with me all the time. All this time, I had been filled with goodness and joy, only I didn't see it.

Of course, I do not hold myself up as a paragon of mental health. But who is? I will always be a misfit in many ways. However, I now realize we are all misfits, at least to ourselves. We all secretly suspect we are freaks, uniquely burdened and especially crazy. Yet that doesn't mean we can't find our place on earth and come to feel loved and welcomed here.

When we learn to face our pain and the pain of others, we start flourishing. The opposite of despair is not a surcease of despair. (Sorrows are all around us.) Rather, its opposite is an explosion of liveliness and joy. Love and light exist deep within us, waiting for us to welcome them into our consciousness and share them with all we meet. My hike up Harney Peak exemplifies this idea.

On a cloudless late-September day, Jim and I climbed Harney Peak, which is the Lakota Sioux's sacred mountain in the Black Hills. I had wanted to do this for thirty years, ever since I read John Neihardt's *Black Elk Speaks*. In the last chapter of that amazing book, Neihardt tells of Black Elk's final hike up Harney Peak. The Sioux holy man had explained to Neihardt that when death approached, a Lakota could climb this mountain to see if the Great Father approved of his life. Rain would fall on those who had the Great Father's approval.

As a young man, Black Elk had a vision that told him how to save his people and homeland from the soldiers and settlers. All of his years, he had worked to fulfill this vision and restore the sacred hoop of life. However, he felt that he had failed and that the sacred hoop was broken.

The day of his climb, Black Elk was an old man. He dressed in

red long-johns, moccasins, war paint and a feathered war head-
dress. Slowly and laboriously, he climbed to the summit. He was
oblivious to the tourists who stared at him. Neihardt teased him
that he should have picked a day with at least one cloud in the sky,
but Black Elk rebuked him, saying that the rain would have nothing to do with the weather.

At the top of the peak, not far from the tourists, the old man lay
down under a blue sky. To his astonishment, Neihardt watched as
a few small clouds immediately formed over Black Elk and a soft
rain began to fall. Black Elk wept with relief. He felt that even
though he had not succeeded in fulfilling his vision, the Great Father was signaling him that he had done his best.

I am embarrassed to confess this, but I wondered if I might see
a sign on the day of my hike. Of course, I didn't tell this to Jim at
the time, and I thoroughly chided myself for my arrogance. Black
Elk and I were not equivalent. He was a holy man who had spoken
to the Great Father every day of his life. I was an ordinary woman
with no deep spiritual traditions of any kind. Still, I could appreciate that this place was sacred. The trail meandered through ancient lodge pole pines and trembling, golden aspens. Mica sparkled
on our path like diamonds. We could see for hundreds of miles, all
of it blue, purple, golden and green.

On the trail we felt a sense of awe, and we could tell other hikers
did, too. When we met others, we were torn between our desire to be
silent and our very American need to be polite and conversational.

As we walked, I tried to imagine what Black Elk might have
thought as he climbed this mountain. Perhaps he remembered his
childhood and his adult experiences. I thought of my grandparents,
aunts and uncles, all dead now. I flashed to my mother's face as she
told me stories on her way to house calls in the country. I could see

my father digging worms in our backyard for a fishing trip. I recalled my childhood times with teachers and friends and with my
siblings who are now scattered like autumn leaves to the four
winds. I thought of my own grown children, my life's work, my
travels and my good times with friends around a campfire.

Several hours later, we hiked the steep last mile to the peak.
Many visitors milled around the stone observation tower. I was
still wondering if it might rain on me or if God would send me a
signal, but I couldn't will myself into any kind of sacred zone while
surrounded by tourists. Maybe Black Elk could, but my spiritual
powers were much weaker.

Still, it was a beautiful morning, with the pine-scented air and
the indigo mountains stretching to the west, north and south. In
the east we could see the uncarved side of Mount Rushmore and,
beyond, the Great Plains. However, after a few minutes, we were
eager to be away from this crowded summit and we turned back
toward the trailhead.

About a half-mile down the trail, Jim and I found a big rock to
sit on while we looked deep into the valley and ate our power bars
and apples. It was here that I allowed myself to feel sorrow that
God had not sent me a sign. I truly had yearned to know if I had
used my time and talents well, as my grandmother Page would
have put it. I also felt stupid and sheepish for having such a grandiose goal. The truth is we postmoderns rarely receive such dramatic validating signals from the universe.

My breathing slowed and I looked around me. The pine siskins
were having a buffet in the tops of trees. The sun illuminated a
patch of cardinal-colored foliage and bronze and silvery grasses,
and a golden eagle coasted on the thermals in the valley below.

I realized that seeing a sign isn't about the power of God, the

Great Father or the Buddha—whatever name you like to use. Seeing a sign is about the spiritual powers and the readiness of the observer. God is everywhere all the time, just beaming out beauty in unimaginable profusion.

Maybe Black Elk had the personal power to change the molecular structure of the sky. But I had a small amount of power. I could see God in the birds, in the perfect grape-sized pinecones and in the cathedrals of stones and trees. These were signs to me that I was a small but welcome part of something immense and timeless. As we climbed down the mountain, I could see God in everything.

STOPPING FOR JOSHUA BELL

Last year Joshua Bell, a world-class violinist, was asked by Gene Weingarten of *The Washington Post* to play near an entrance to a Washington, D.C., subway station. His performance was videotaped so that the reactions of commuters could be studied. Bell selected what he considered the most beautiful pieces of music ever written. He stood for hours in a busy station playing one piece after another. Only a few people even noticed him, and at the end of the day, he had collected less than thirty dollars in tips.

Yet all the children who passed him wanted to watch and listen. On the video we can see them tugging on their parents' arms and turning their faces toward Bell even as they are being led away.

One woman did recognize Bell, and as thousands of fellow commuters rushed by, she listened in amazement to his entire performance. Mostly, though, his playing wafted past ears that, in a workday rush, had no room for music. Of course, no one was expecting him in a subway, and many people have no exposure to classical music. Still, they missed an opportunity for transcendence.

Since I read about this experiment, it has become a metaphor for me. I have asked myself, "Do I want to rush past Joshua Bell?"

Long ago in Texas, on the fishing dock with my father, I became aware of the power of a moment. That night I realized that time can be conceptualized in different ways and that it can be stopped and expanded into something grander. The Greeks knew this with their distinction between chronological time, *kronos*, and sacred time, *kairos*. Just as with energy, time can be both a wave and a particle, something continuous and something discrete. My idea is that moments are discrete time, complete in themselves and utterly distinct from the habit-bound wave time in which we all live much of our lives. While minutes are earthbound and can be measured, moments both merge with eternal time and exist outside time altogether.

Not all minutes are created equal and only a few become moments. We tend to greet every minute with demands such as: "I want this. I don't want this. I want more of this. I want less of that." We have ideas about what our minutes should or should not be. We want sunshine or rain, quiet or company, work or rest. We are such yearning organisms.

Yet there is a sense in which many of us are fighting for our lives. We are struggling to be present for our own experiences. There is no more important task before us, or anything that could bring us more love and joy.

If we are lucky, occasionally we experience a sparkling moment when we break out of our trance of self and are fully present. Sometimes these lead to epiphanies, which present us with aha moments of new understanding. Or our thoughts simply may be "Isn't this wonderful?" or "Isn't life amazingly rich and complicated?" Or even, "Doesn't this look beautiful or taste delicious?"

What makes moments distinct is that we are celebrating what actually is.

Most people experience a few such moments—perhaps on their honeymoon or when their children are born. Some people who survive into their nineties never inhabit a moment; others die young after enjoying thousands. The number of moments we experience in our lifetimes is what makes us rich or poor. They are what we want to remember on our deathbeds, which, parenthetically, is often a time when people enjoy beautiful moments.

Psychologist Abraham Maslow called moments "peak experiences" and argued that they were often transformative. Many activists can describe the moment that inspired them to dedicate their lives to a cause. I know a high school girl who watched a film on the child soldiers of Uganda. Natalia was so moved by the film that she worked to share it with all the churches and schools in our town. She collected money for the child soldiers who were in trauma rehabilitation. Before she was out of high school, she was making a film about the Sudanese refugees in our town. Seeing *Invisible Children* at school had changed her life.

A farmer told me of watching his son splashing after minnows and polliwogs in a creek on his land. As he stood there, he realized that he and other farmers were poisoning the water with their fertilizers. They were depleting the water table with inefficient irrigation systems. He wanted to make the creek safe for his son and for his grandsons-to-be and for all his neighbors' children as well. This man walked home with his boy and called the extension office for information on sustainable agriculture.

As a therapist, I shared many moments with my clients. I recall one with Wanda, a large, plain thirty-year-old woman from a small town near Lincoln. At first, she had seemed a rather quiet, bland person, but as she slowly opened up and told me about her life, I realized she was remarkable.

When Wanda was eight, her mother died of breast cancer. She lived with her father, who was a long-distance trucker. When he was home, he was a taciturn TV watcher who had little interest in his daughter. Her mother had been an only child, and her dad was estranged from his family. After her mother's death, she was pretty much on her own.

Wanda cooked, cleaned and did her school work. Her only companion was her dad's old hunting dog, whom she dearly loved. She attended church with her girlfriends on Sundays. Elementary school was lonely because she had no parent to come to programs and help with events. She liked high school better because of the activities. She was in Sewing Club and Pep Club, but she had never been asked on a date. She cried when she told me that.

After high school, she was hired to work in a dairy, and her real life began. She liked the physical work with animals. She grew close to her coworkers, and for the first time in her life, she was going out to eat and into the city to see movies and concerts. She had a little money for clothes and musical recordings. She sometimes watched the boss's children, whom she came to love. They called her Aunt Wanda.

Wanda wasn't dating and didn't feel attractive. However, as we talked, I realized she had everything she needed to be loved. I remember the day she discovered that. She wondered if anyone would ever love her, and I asked her to name all the people she loved. She surprised herself with the length of the list. I asked softly, "Do they love you back?"

After a while she said, "I guess I am already lovable." She smiled, her eyes glistening with tears.

Moments can be restorative. I once worked in California and stayed in a hotel surrounded by malls, interstates and parking lots. The hotel managed to be noisy and sterile at the same time. My room was dark and gloomy, and I couldn't walk outside because there were no sidewalks. However, as I entered the parking lot to catch a ride to my speech, I smelled wisteria. Cascading from a nearby chain-link fence were fragrant, glorious vines with the purple flowers hanging like bunches of grapes. I walked over to the clump and sank my face in wisteria. As I gulped in its aroma, I felt a sense of grace.

Moments bring great joy. My friend Margie writes poems describing walking her daughter's dog, baking a chocolate pie or flirting with her husband at a traffic light. She is gifted at being present for what most of us would see as ordinary minutes. Margie jokes she has so much fun that she should be charged an excess tax.

Another man I know, who makes his rather meager living guiding canoe trips, says often, "It's all about joy." Indeed, he has the skills to live his life as a process in which every minute counts. Oliver Sacks wrote of a woman who after her brain surgery was greatly changed. She became continually positive and upbeat. The woman called herself a "joyologist." I want to be a joyologist myself.

My friend Jan and I challenge each other in happiness contests. We tend to do this on dull gray days in February or on mornings when we have tedious work ahead. Late in the day, we'll e-mail each other our entries. It isn't that we do anything special, but rather that we appreciate what happens. Our lists are simple: I made some delicious turkey noodle soup. I bought hyacinths at the grocery store. I walked in the snow at sunset or read a good book by the fire. I had a phone call with my daughter and listened to geese flying overhead. When we have these contests, we create our own good days.

Jim's bandmate Reynold once created a moment for a club filled with friends. The Fabtones were onstage at the Zoo Bar performing a rollicking version of the Sam and Dave soul song "Soothe Me." Reynold, who drums and sings, said during a pause in the song, "I can sense there is a lot of tension in this room. It's Friday night. We've all had long weeks. Now is the time to kick back. We need to soothe each other." Then he instructed the audience to turn to their neighbor, any neighbor, and give them a neck rub while the band rocked into another verse and chorus of "Soothe Me." The crowd did as they were told and, believe me, Reynold created a moment.

When we radiate joy, we attract it. On my best days, when I am out running errands, I try to really look into the faces of the people I encounter. That involves making eye contact and, in my heart, wishing them well. I'll try to beam happiness their way. When I am capable of this, people often respond by beaming back. Their facial muscles will soften and their voices will be lighter and warmer. This meeting can be a matter of milliseconds, but it turns an interaction into a moment.

Of course, I don't walk around joy-filled every day. I am still impatient and easily rattled by stress. I have days when I am lost in a fog of self-pity or soul-draining misery. Many mornings I still wake up in a sour mood, and I can ruminate over a casual remark to the point of absurdity. Even now, my fallback expression is a deep and furrowed frown. I continue to hold my rank as the worst Buddhist in the world. But I am more capable of inviting joy into my life.

We all underestimate our need for joy. If we are not careful, we live as if our schedules are our lives. We cross one thing after another off the list. At the end of the day, we have completed our chores, but we haven't necessarily been present for our own experiences.

Just before she died in 2004, Elisabeth Kübler-Ross was interviewed for National Public Radio. She said she was at peace with herself. Her body had worn out and she was ready for death. She believed she had led a good, productive life and would go to heaven. I was struck by one remark she made. "I'll dance among the stars, but I wish I had danced more down below."

We are what we pay attention to. Sadly, most of the time we are not attending to the world or ourselves. Psychologists estimate we have sixty thousand to seventy thousand thoughts a day, 99 percent of which are more or less what we thought yesterday. Our habits run our lives. Most of the time, we are phoning it in.

Of course, much of our automatic behavior is functional. Understandably, we attempt to screen out ugliness and coarseness. We avoid advertisements, noise pollution or the smell and sight of dog poop on the sidewalk. We don't necessarily feel the need to monitor our toaster carefully every time we toast a piece of bread. Yet too much of this automatic behavior and we become automatons. We don't notice the waving baby or the taste of a ripe mango. We don't really see our coworkers' faces or hear the wind in the treetops.

In all my years as a therapist, I have never seen people as rushed and distracted as they are now. Everyone is too busy all the time. We have become a nation of multitaskers. By definition, multitasking means the mind is divided and not fully focused on any one event. A very simple definition of mindfulness is doing one thing at a time. If we are planting some turnips, we are doing it properly. If we are reading to a child, that is all we are doing.

I have a long history of doing two or three or seventeen things at once. I am cooking, but planning my next road trip. I am talking on the phone, but wondering if I have a can of tuna handy for lunch. I am bird-watching, but worrying if I have offended someone. I am walking, but even as I smell the French lilacs in the air and notice the heron on the lake, I am thinking of presidential politics. Yet slowly I am discovering that life is best when I am one place at a time; that is to say that when I am cooking, I am cooking. Well, okay, maybe stirring and listening to the radio, but I am not planning a Father's Day party for the extended family.

Sometimes inhabiting the moment is simple indeed. We hear Louis Armstrong or Chopin on the radio. We taste our lover's kisses, the pomegranate juice or the salt air. We smell the sage or the jasmine blossom.

Animals can pull us into the moment. One of the reasons pets are so popular is that when we are with them, we share their pleasure in being here now. Pets do not live in clock time, and they allow us to rest from chronological time. We join them in older, animal rhythms.

On winter nights, Jim and I sit in our recliners and look out onto the snow and the lake. We wait for our local fox to appear. When he comes, he runs along our south fence toward the lake. He is the color of a shadow and his fur fluffs out like feathers. He trots onto the dam, runs in tight circles, then pounces on whatever prey is available. Within a few seconds he is gone. Afterward, having seen the fox, we are as giddy as children.

Most people respond to wild animals the way we do. I think it is because, deep within us, we carry something far more ancient than human thoughts. Animal spottings, whether of eagles, grizzlies or dolphins, remind us of our ancient selves. Primordial appreciates primordial. We have a moment to connect to something older than our culture, our history and our short lives.

Because children live in the present, we can join them in fresh experiences. Until they are educated away from living in the moment, that is their natural place. Just recently, I drove my grandchildren to the Ozarks for a family reunion. Eating a chocolate doughnut at our Days Inn and thinking about swimming with her newfound cousins, three-year-old Claire said, "My heart is snuggling inside me." Then she realized this didn't quite express what she was experiencing in her chest. She said, "My heart feels very big right now." Her life was not so complicated that she couldn't recognize the physical sensations of joy.

Once my grandson A.B. said, "I love you," to me on the telephone; I responded in kind. He said urgently, "Nonna, you don't understand, I love you right now." He could perceive that he was alive to his experience of love in a way that, at the minute, I wasn't.

Another time when A.B. stayed with us, he came out to the living room long after his bedtime. I was reading, but instead of sending him back to bed, I suggested we cuddle and look at the full moon. A.B. settled into my lap wearing his Spiderman pajamas and holding his ever-present bird book. I showed him the mountains of the moon and asked him if he had ever seen mountains. He said yes, in the Sandhills, he had seen mountains. Then he noticed the lights across the lake and whispered, "Nonna, I want to live in that beautiful city." He was looking at a ball field lit for a night game. For the first time, those lights seemed wondrous to me.

When we surround ourselves with beauty, we are likely to experience a moment. We have our "peak experiences" on the beach or prairie, in a mountain meadow or beside a river. We experience moments at concerts, art galleries or the theater. However, most of us can't get to these places on a regular basis. We are encased in offices, crowded apartments, commuter trains, highways and shopping malls. To create moments in our daily lives, we must have a new set of skills for making magic out of the ordinary. Psychology and all the great spiritual traditions teach these skills.

Fortunately, the more moments we find, the more we learn to find them. The process is not unlike being receptive to the muse. Artists know that to access their creativity, they must somehow be curious and attentive. They learn not to reject the small openings, the little tugs on the sleeve, the miniature portals that open into something vast and immediate.

To practice living in the moment, I play around with writing haikus, short poems that describe a physical reality, such as snow falling on a plum branch or snails sizzling in a pan, and offer a philosophical/emotional reflection. Actually, I don't so much write haikus as discover them. When I stop my monkey mind, take a few deep breaths and look around, a haiku will fall into my lap. It isn't good poetry, but it helps me learn to be in the now.

With a certain attitude, everything is significant. With an "Are we there yet?" mentality, we are doomed. I've seen this in national parks. In a matter of minutes, some tourists will drive into a parking area, jump out of their cars, take a picture and be on their way again. No one has taught them that to enjoy a natural place, one must sit down, be quiet and look, simply look, for a long time. My own egregious example of this is a deeply entrenched rule that I cannot rest or relax until all my work is done. What a deal. I could die of old age before I have met all my responsibilities and done all my chores.

We all live surrounded by temple bells. It can be the ding of an e-mail, the sight of a taxi, a seed pod twirling to the ground or the aroma of coffee. I've coached myself to breathe deeply at stop signs and to be aware of my thoughts, my body and my emotions. Most of the time, I forget to do this, but the one in a thousand times when I actually succeed, I enjoy it. I feel calm and relaxed and I drive on refreshed. I should add a word of caution to the reader: Don't do this if you are too easily distracted. Occasionally, I have been wakened from my reverie by a honking horn or someone shouting and giving me the finger.

I spend much of my time mired in habitual thinking and monkey mind, but I am now aware that our ordinary ways of seeing are but curtains that cover the radiance all around us. When I am fortunate enough to see that radiance, I am comforted. I am less frightened and more optimistic. I trust the universe and my place in it. I do not fear death for myself or for others. I sense that ultimately everything will be all right for all of us. The universe seems to be much kinder than I ever imagined.

I hear stories from my friends that inspire me to create yet more moments. A musician named Chris told me about playing music in Kansas. He stayed at the home of an elderly patron of the arts. This woman sponsored many musicians and invited them to stay in her third-floor apartment. Most refused because the woman was a big talker, but Chris enjoyed her conversations. She was intelligent and kind and told him incredible stories. The last time Chris played in her town, this woman was in the hospital dying, but she insisted on returning to her home to host Chris. They had a wonderful last visit. She told him how much his friendship and visits had meant to her. Chris created some sacred time with this woman. He had stopped for Joshua Bell.

Another friend takes pictures of ordinary minutes that become moments under her compassionate attention. Recently I attended her father-in-law's funeral. As is now common, we watched a slideshow of pictures of the departed. But this display was different. Over the years, my friend had taken many pictures of him doing his ordinary activities. We saw photos of him doing a crossword puzzle, walking with his wife, feeding his birds, digging up bulbs, mowing his grass, making coffee, washing his car and reading stories to his grandchildren. With these photos, my friend had sanctified her father-in-law's days.

My friend Cindy told me about her Mother's Day the year her mother died. She was with her mother in the nursing home all morning and ate a terrible lunch with her. Her mother was incoherent and confused and the morning was, as Cindy put it, "thoroughly horrid." Cindy came home and said to her husband, "Take me on a car ride. I just want to get out of town."

They packed a picnic and headed for a nearby wild animal park. As they drove into the park, they saw a car stop for a few minutes and then drive on. They pulled over to see what was happening and spotted a pregnant deer about to give birth. They waited patiently and witnessed the birth of the fawn. They watched as the doe licked off the fawn, who then stood and shook herself. Cindy said, "At that moment, my day totally changed." They were lucky to see the deer, but they had orchestrated their good fortune by slowing down.

Every now and then, we humans are gifted with mythic days that rearrange the deep structure of our being and transform our lives. These kinds of days can't be orchestrated, but they are more likely to happen under certain conditions—in beautiful places, with loved ones and when we are at peace. Under these conditions, we may be treated to a symphony of moments.

In July, Jim and I traveled with our friend and office partner from Nebraska to Copper Mountain, Colorado, to stay in Jan's family condo. Nine months earlier, Jan's husband, Jerry, had a heart attack in this condo. He had been life-flighted to Denver, and a week later died during open-heart surgery.

Jan wanted us to return to Colorado with her, ostensibly to make a financial decision about keeping this condo. However, on a deeper level, Jan realized this condo was the one place in her world where time had stood still. Since last September, her life in Nebraska had moved on. But at the condo, Jerry was as he had been on their last visit. In the odd logic of the heart, Jan could feel close to him there.

Jan, Jim and I have worked together as therapists for thirty years. We have nurtured each other's children, shared Thanksgiving dinners, and had decades of staff meetings and trips to professional development workshops. In all the years we've been partners, we have not had a tense hour or a harsh word between us. Even as I write this, it sounds too good to be true, but it is true. Jim and I were honored to accompany Jan on this pilgrimage.

Now I must say this: Jan and I vacation in different Colorados. Jim and I like to backpack into a wilderness area, find an isolated spot near a creek and stay out of range of humans as long as we can. Jan likes hot showers, coffee shops, soft beds and shopping. Copper Mountain reminds her of family ski trips, whereas, with its crowds, shops and music piped through the trees, it reminds me of a mall.

We arrived Sunday night, and Monday we acclimated to the altitude. Tuesday, July Fourth, we rented bikes and rode around Lake Dillon. As we biked through Frisco, we came upon the helipad where Jerry had been life-flighted to an ICU in Denver. The shock of that sight almost knocked Jan off her bike and, for some time afterward, left her speechless.

On Wednesday, we woke early and drove over Berthoud Pass to the Indian Peaks Wilderness Area. We parked at the Monarch Lake trailhead and hiked through aspens past the blue mirror of the lake into the pines and snow-bent cedars. We followed tumbling Cascade Creek with its waterfalls cut through cathedral-sized boulders.

At first we talked about the natural beauty and about the possibilities for bears, rockslides and mountain lions, but as the day progressed we grew quieter. We spotted trout in the creek's dark, clear pools and hiked by columbines the size of saucers. We picked tiny strawberries and admired the wild roses, mountain asters, the Indian paintbrush and salmon-colored pasqueflowers. Flowers dotted the meadows like jewels on a soft green shawl, and butterflies flew from one flower to another as if to call our attention to each one's particular beauty. Hummingbirds buzzed us.

At one point, we heard, then saw, a tree crash in the forest about three hundred yards away from us. Actually, what we heard was a loud crack that could have been a gunshot, a rockslide or thunder. We froze and looked at each other. None of us knew which way to run. As the tree began its descent, it crashed through other trees, loudly and quickly at first, but then more slowly and softly. By the time it reached the forest floor, it shushed down like a baby being put into a cradle.

We rested for a while beside the downed tree. We were not the spring chickens we used to be. I puffed and panted more than when I first hiked this trail twenty years earlier at age thirty-eight. Even Jim, who is a marathon runner, wasn't bounding over boulders the way he once had. I could almost see our younger selves walking beside us.

When I am in beautiful surroundings, I am always reminded of people I love who are far away in time or place. Beauty dissolves boundaries. The living and the dead are not separated. Magic seems more possible, as does resurrection. As I walked in that green, quiet place, I remembered my last days with my mother. When she lay dying in an ICU in a hospital in Kansas by the slow, muddy Republican River, I comforted her by pretending we were camping beside a mountain stream. I whispered that the sound of her machines gurgling was the sound of a cold, fast-running Colorado creek. We held hands, counted stars and listened to the wind through the pines.

The ghosts of Jim's parents hovered nearby as well. His mother had died the year before, and his father lay near death in a nursing home. I sensed the presence of our children and old friends who had been on this trail with us before. I could feel the ghosts of Porky and Bess, the porcupines we named after they woke us our first night in this wilderness twenty years ago. They had slipped into our campsite to lick toothpaste off the rocks near our tent. We heard a snorting outside our tent, and we fearfully opened our window, turned on our flashlight and found ourselves face to face with an indolent porcupine couple.

As I thought of other times, I knew that Jerry was with us, too. We had come to banish grief, and for the most part, we had succeeded. But we hadn't banished memory. In fact, we were flooded with memories of Jerry and of so many others. Not only did we feel a kinship to each other and the natural world, but we felt a kinship to all those who had lived and who would be born.

At the falls, we stopped for a rest and lunch. Jim and Jan hiked on to the site of our first camp. I had injured my knee on a previous mountain climb and it was throbbing and swelling. I stayed behind at a spot close to Cascade Falls. I meditated on the sounds, the spray, the light and the coldness of the water. Every moment of watching was a lesson in time. To try to stop time or to hold on to the past is like trying to stop a waterfall.

Then I spotted the ouzel—a nondescript gray-brown bird about the size of a barn swallow. Ouzels live only in remote areas by waterfalls, and their outstanding characteristic is that they can dive into the rapids, whose pressure would splinter a canoe, and emerge with a small fish. As this ouzel darted in and out of the falls, I followed her path to a large daubed nest about three stories up on the rock face. Two chicks waited for those little fish. Only their orange beaks were visible when their mother appeared with dinner. Once, when the mother was delayed, they peeked out and cheeped so loudly that I could hear them above the roar of the falls. I wondered: "How long in evolutionary time did it take to find the exact set of notes that can be heard over a waterfall? Have ouzels occupied this site since the Midwest was a great inland lake, since before the Native Americans came?"

When Jim and Jan returned, they brought the vertebrae of an elk, three rocks delivered by the last glacier and a porcupine quill, perhaps from a grandchild of Porky and Bess. We watched the hardworking ouzel feed her young, we passed around bread, cheese and apples, and we talked about time. The waterfall itself was formed by millions of years of water trickling across stone. And what are we made of, but the same stardust that made the rock, the ouzel, the aspen and the elk.

Jim and I met Jan in our twenties. I had long, blond hair, a new Ph.D., a first-grade son, and a baby daughter. Jan hired Jim to work at a mental health clinic in rural Nebraska. I commuted to Lincoln to teach. Jan was gorgeous, lively and fun-loving, with a handsome, witty husband and an important job as director of a seven-county mental health system. She and Jerry had yet to become the parents of two children.

Now all of our children are grown. Jerry is dead and Jim has hearing loss after all those years in bands. My hair is gray and my hands are freckled with age spots. Jan is still beautiful (all her wrinkles must be on the inside), but she has deepened over the years, as have we. Time is the great teacher of equanimity, even in the face of death. As we age, trees crash all around us. They rest on the forest floor, where saplings sprout up.

Slowly and almost silently, we walked three hours back to the trailhead. There we found someone to photograph us. Tired and hot, we limped to the car in a faraway parking lot. My knee had swollen to the size of a grapefruit, and Jan had blisters on her feet. We were thirsty and achy, yet so jubilant that we stayed in a happiness trance all the way across misty Berthoud Pass and into Copper Mountain.

That wilderness hike was orchestrated for awe, the universal elixir for healing. Always I am transformed by a venture into the great green heart of the world. Cue up the forests, waterfalls, physical exertion and freedom from time. Add in a few marmots, cascades of wildflowers, a red fox, a grove of quaking aspen and a nest of baby ouzels. Beautiful moments are bound to happen.

When I was younger, I thought such experiences were about perfection, the hike without scratches, the sky without clouds, but now I see that mythic days require the swollen knee, the blistered feet, the early afternoon cloudburst and even a little fear. The mountain lion tracks enhance the beauty of the columbine. Embedded in the concept of mythic is the concept of overcoming, of pushing beyond ordinary limits. Awe is the aspen curling upward from a cup of soil in the rock; it is the pasqueflower nodding in the snow.

Pain, as well as beauty, is necessary to give us perspective. We can place our suffering against the backdrop of time and allow our nagging little egos to rest in the great verdant container of the timeless. We feel smaller, yet connected to something bigger and grander. Our place in time is but a sliver of a nanosecond against the great backdrop of galaxies exploding. Yet this knowledge is comforting. To know one's place is to be at home, and whether home is the womb, a mountain canyon or a meditation room, it is the best of all places to be.

Of course, being me, I want to take this experience back to Nebraska, to bottle it and drink it like a tonic whenever I am blue or too caught up in the everyday. I cannot do this, of course. However, I can create a similar moment by meditating or watching the moon rise above my masthead pine. The next time I am stuck in traffic or forced to be in a mall or airport, I can feel grateful that places like Cascade Creek Canyon exist. I can remember this hike and exhale.

When I return to Lincoln, I tell my grandchildren about the trip. Since they don't know what a waterfall looks like, I describe the mother-of-pearl spray, the icy water and the roar of water falling over boulders bigger than their church. They grow wide-eyed at imagined waterfalls. I explain about the ouzel fishing in the falls and her spaceship-shaped mud nest high up on the cliff, higher even than the roof of their church. I tell them about the chicks' orange beaks and their peeps that can be heard over the sounds of the falls. I describe how they impatiently pulled the silver fish from their mother's mouth. Then I present them with rocks I carried down from that site. Aidan clutches his to his chest, runs to his dad and says in a hushed voice, "Dad, I have here in my hands a rock from a waterfall with an ouzel."

As I talk to them, I think, "It goes on." That is life's great sorrow and greatest solace. It goes on. A star dies and another is formed in a celestial cycle of birth and death. One mountain crumbles to sand and another explodes into being. An ouzel nest may last ten thousand years, while I will be dust in a hundred. When I truly understand, I know there is only the illusion of time, or rather, that we live both within and outside of time, and that we can be grateful for both experiences.

WHERE I AM NOW

(2008)

B y now I am grateful that on a dreary November day, in a dirty café in the northeast, I tasted that memorable bowl of chili. At that crucial moment, I understood that my life wasn't working. I didn't know where I was going, but I couldn't stay where I was. I could no longer ignore my own anguish. Pain was what caused me to open my life into a larger container.

The two hardest times of my life were my first-grade year without my mother and the winter of 2002. In the latter case, I had much more control. I wasn't a child. I could think like an adult and I could make good choices. After my meltdown, I learned new skills and gained insights into my personality. Meditation showed me many things I didn't want to see—my neediness and my harshness with my self, my lack of courage and my vulnerability. But it also showed me my basic goodness and my own powers of resilience.

It is easy for me to understand why I wrote this book. Pain, curiosity and a desire for truth motivated me to examine my life with a thorough and thoughtful process. The more difficult ques-

tion is why I am sharing my personal struggles with readers. I am
a private, self-protective person who is now broadcasting my vulnerabilities. What possessed me to promulgate my story?

I believe that if readers see something of themselves in me, I
may be useful. I may help readers feel less alone and damaged, just
as I helped myself with these goals. We all share similar journeys.
We live through childhoods filled with ups and downs. We share
houses with people who both love us and make us miserable. We
pass developmental milestones, build identities and see them
change. We fail miserably and we accomplish important goals. We
make the best of it. We take turns being the afflicted and the comforter. We experience a crisis and realize our old ways are not
working. We stumble around lost and unhappy, only to see the
light, find our new path and move forward. This is our universal
human story.

Winston Churchill said, "We haven't journeyed all this way because we are made of sugar candy." Every one of us possesses what
we need to flourish. None of us are doomed. Many people have told
me that the low point in their lives was also the high point. That,
retrospectively, the moment when they heard they had cancer or
that they lost their job was their worst and best moment. Ideally,
people rise to the occasion and afterward they say, "I never thought
I had it in me." A Vietnam veteran once told me that he experienced
almost no stress. When he had a root canal surgery, an IRS audit or
a plumbing problem, his reaction was, "Hell, I've been to Vietnam.
This is nothing."

I still consider myself to be a world-class stress monkey. I continue to be restless and distractible. I have almost as much trouble
sitting still now as I did in elementary school. I can be so mired in
the future or past that I miss witnessing something miraculous in

the present. Sometimes I wonder if I will fully inhabit my life before it is time to leave it behind.

The major change in me is that I don't resist that agitation. One morning recently, I woke up and realized I was thinking about a dozen different topics at once. I thanked my mind for being exactly as it was. I told myself that, over the years, my hot hot hot brain has accomplished a great deal for me and for other people.

My demons hang around the way they always have, but I no longer fight with them every time they show up. Sometimes I welcome them into my heart. I spend less time photoshopping my inner life. I can better tolerate my own lack of perfection and ride the waves of my moods. I am less fearful and shameful.

The women in my family taught me to care for others, but I taught myself to be good to me. I learned to ask myself a new question: What would make me happy? No virtue is absolute. Just as it is important to work for others, it is good to relax and enjoy one's own experiences.

For the rest of my life I will wrestle with questions about when to care for myself and for others. I am fortunate, in that every day I have dozens of opportunities to help other people. I can read and recommend books, write letters of recommendation, make speeches, serve on boards, be an advocate for various groups, care for refugees and immigrants, teach graduate students, speak for good causes and write in ways that are useful to the world. I am deeply grateful that I can be of service, but I am also aware that if I don't watch out, I can become exhausted and depleted.

Recently I had a dream in which I walked outside my house into a sky pulsing with stars. Nebulae were throbbing, comets coursed the dome of the sky, the Milky Way was a white river of light, and stars of all colors were falling like fireworks. Jim was already outside looking at the sky. He said, "Get a blanket and come on out. We'll lie in the grass and watch the stars all night." Of course, I agreed and eagerly ran for a blanket. Then I heard the phone ring. I remembered I had promised to call someone. I had a fax coming in, and I realized the cat wanted to be petted. Even as I desperately desired to look at the night sky, I was held back by my duties and chores. I became increasingly panicky as I realized in my dream that the sun was coming up and I still hadn't made it to the blanket on the grass.

I didn't need a psychologist to help me interpret that dream. Its meaning was clear. Seize the hour. Don't miss an opportunity to enjoy beauty. Give yourself permission to throw away the to-do list and lie down in the tall grasses.

After all these years of trying to improve myself, I have actually improved. I have gained skills in putting the ups and downs of daily life in perspective. When someone is grumpy with me, I no longer feel quite so anxious. Recently Zeke chided me for letting three-year-old Claire have too many breath mints. Normally, the exasperation of my adult children upsets me. This time, I could just let it go, and a few minutes later he was giving me a hug. Recently, after a day of turmoil that seemed to last a hundred years, I was able to tell myself, "Some days are better than others." That realization for me, who expects every day to be productive and amazing, was an epiphany.

I have learned grand things, such as how to moment, and small things, such as how to stay in bed for a few minutes and relax when I wake up. I am better able to sort out the difference between "That's life" and "That's nuts." Intensity is no longer my most prominent trait. Most of the time I can avoid reacting to situations in a way that makes them worse. More and more often I can find that quiet place inside myself that allows me to be present for myself and others. I am not depressed and I sleep as well as most people. My health is again excellent in all ways.

Occasionally, I still experience that squishy feeling that signals to me that I am vulnerable. However, generally I don't panic when I feel it. I have discovered ways to soothe myself. What I had viewed as my pathology, I realize now is simply the human experience. My flaws, weaknesses and suffering are my calling card into the parlor of the human race. As an outsider, I've come to feel part of the whole human family.

I am grateful for my crises of confidence and for the healing process that followed. I thank the universe that I could journey into Buddhism, with its wisdom about the human psyche and its practices in acceptance and self-awareness. I feel deeply fortunate that when I most needed it, I could rest. During my years of relative quiet, daily meditation, reading and reflection, I was able to tamp down my arousal system and rebuild my life. I don't think I'll ever again feel as fragile as I did that winter.

I received two gifts the long, harsh winter of 2007. I learned some things about my father and about myself the year I was six. As the snow fell day after day and the wind rattled our windows, I watched Ken Burns's documentary *The War*, about World War Two, and I read *The Coldest Winter*, David Halberstam's excellent book on the Korean conflict. These two works gave me some understanding of my father as an adult and of his experiences just before I was born and when I was a little girl. He had talked very little about the war; mostly he had told us a few funny stories about his Army buddies. I had understood nothing about his true experiences.

In *The War*, we see the fighting through the eyes of ordinary soldiers. As I watched the series, I observed scenes of men lying

blown apart on beaches in Okinawa or the Philippines, or hud-
dling in mud, hungry and afraid. I heard old men talk of troop
transports, hand-to-hand combat, isolation, lack of supplies and
the horror of seeing young men suffer and die. As though he had
written his script personally for me, Burns included a tribute to
medics like my dad. He told viewers that when men were injured
they called out, "Medic! Medic!" Without weapons, the medics
ran into the fray to carry soldiers out of the fighting and do what
they could to help them. Medics saw the most damaged bodies and
the hardest fighting. Burns called them unsung heroes.

Halberstam writes about the Korean conflict as a series of enormous military and political mistakes. It was a war so badly bungled
that it was in almost everyone's best interest to pretend it never
happened. *The Coldest Winter* brings it all back—General Doug-
las MacArthur's megalomania and incompetence, the frostbite
from 40 below zero temperatures, the slaughter of American soldiers along mountain roads in North Korea and the well-led and
well-outfitted Chinese troops dressed in warm white coats that allowed them to be invisible in the snow when reconnaissance planes
flew over.

As I read this book, I thought of my father's years in that conflict.
He must have been caught up in the nightmare fighting in the
mountains of North Korea. He must have buried frozen bodies in
the hard ground and wondered if he would survive all the misman-
agement by the Army headquarters in Tokyo. As Dad sat in foxholes
and ate K-rations, he must have thought constantly of his wife and
children in a warm house with plenty of food and hot water. No
doubt he worried about my mother handling everything by herself.
Surely he missed us every day, but especially on holidays and our
birthdays. How could I not have understood this earlier?

Shortly after Dad's stint in the South Pacific, I was born. When he came home from Korea, I was five. That is when he, Jake and I moved to Missouri. He must have been damaged and traumatized by his war years. He and my mother may not have coped well with his reentry into family life. However, like many GIs, he buried his pain. He worked, attended college and took care of Jake and me. He helped our family pretend that nothing had really happened to him.

It has taken me many decades to put together this story of my father, and I couldn't have done it without Burns and Halberstam. At last I realize how much of my father's adult life was about sacrifice—for our country and for our family. When he was twenty-two, he left his beloved Ozarks to risk his life fighting Japan in World War Two. He rejoined the Army in 1948 so that he could help my mother pay for medical school. He spent those dreadful years in Korea; then he spent the rest of his life following his wife from town to town across the Great Plains.

Finally, as an adult and a psychologist, I grasp that his whole life was affected by his years in terrible places. I wish I could talk to him now. I would say, "Dad, I am sorry. I didn't understand. I know you did your best. Thank you for taking care of us all. Thank you. Thank you." As I am writing this, Jim walks into my study and asks, "Why is your face covered with tears?"

This same winter, my son and his wife traveled to China for sixteen days. Jim and I devoted ourselves to their children. We read to them, took them to a play and a gymnastics meet, invited over other kids to keep them company and played endless card games. In general, Claire and A.B. did fine. Six-year-old Kate was the one who suffered the most. She didn't want to leave my side. Several nights she cried at bedtime. She talked a great deal about

missing her mother and grew distraught when her parents called.
I bought her a pretty music box to help her "not be so sad," but the
next day she said that it didn't really help at all. Clearly, she missed
her mother incessantly. She felt squishy.

As I watched Kate, I thought of myself as a girl. Kate was separated from her mother for only sixteen days. She stayed with her
grandparents in familiar settings. She had someone to sit beside
her every night as she cried. Yet she suffered. How much greater
must my own suffering have been. I can't remember most of what
happened to me the year I was six, but feeling such love and pro-
tectiveness toward Kate opened my heart toward myself as a girl.

Everything changes. A rich life is experienced in contrasts. After a period of reflection, it is time for some company. For a few
years, I lived a more solitary life than usual for me. I have always
loved to be with others. I liked being a carhop or the swim team
snack bar manager. I liked potlucks, card parties and campouts
with groups of friends. I organized the family reunions and dinner
parties, the Sunday afternoon walks and the bird-watching safaris
for out-of-town guests. I liked teaching and doing therapy. Until
my meltdown, my life had been filled with other people who gave
my life joy and meaning. As I grew and healed myself, I energeti-
cally reentered the world.

I need to clarify that the differences between my life as an in-
trovert and as an extrovert are subtle. I've always spent time alone
reading or out-of-doors, and during my years of self-study, I've delivered dozens of speeches, written three books, worked with refugees, taught in writers' workshops, traveled and experienced many
happy times with my family and friends. Now that I am turning
back toward a more outgoing life, I'll continue to meditate and
save time for walks and my hammock.

I know the exact moment I realized this sense of turning. The day after I finished my first draft of this book, I felt an instantaneous wash of relief and elation. My years of isolation and self-involvement were over. My mood turned jubilant.

The next day, Jim's band was playing a Friday Afternoon Club at the Zoo Bar. I knew my daughter and many of my friends would be there, but I chose instead to take in the movie *Into Great Silence*, about the Carthusian monks who take a vow of silence and rarely even share a meal together. The movie was filmed at an isolated monastery near Grenoble, France. Even as I walked into the theater, I wondered if I was making a mistake. Dancing to the Fabtones and laughing with friends sounded more enticing.

However, I bought my ticket and found a seat in the almost empty theater. I endeavored to enjoy this almost three-hour-long movie with no sound track and almost no speech. Actually, the main sound during this movie was the snoring of the man behind me who would doze off, grunt loudly, then fall forward, gasp, wake up and start his cycle again.

I settled in to watch scenes of monks kneeling in silent prayer in their small prayer cubicles. For ten minutes, I observed the hands of a novice as he chopped up celery. For a long while, I watched an expressionless old monk shave the head of a younger monk who was also without expression. Then I watched as the barber slowly swept the hair off the floor and put it in a wastebasket. One repeating motif was of a towel blowing in the breeze. Another was of the clouds in the sky above the monastery.

The silence and pacing of this beautifully executed movie were designed to help us move into the rhythms and experiences of the monks. At a different time, I might have found this film deeply meaningful. However, that Friday night, I was restless. I missed my friends and the immediacy and energy of live music. I wanted to be hugging people and catching up on the news. Finally, during a long scene in which a monk was dusting furniture, I walked out of the theater into the bright afternoon light. When I told my husband about my experience, he broke into a grin and said, "I have my Mary back."

The next night, I accompanied Jim to a bluegrass gig for a block party. A hundred people sat on lawn chairs on a beautiful June evening. I helped myself to a plate of smoked turkey and salads and poured myself a glass of wine. I sat with my friends and talked as the lightning bugs blinked on. As Jim's band played, I heard about Kim's new job, Kathy's daughter's move to Minneapolis and Chris's son's progress in college.

At breaks, Jim sat by me holding my hand. I soaked it all in— the toddlers chasing each other, the neighbors dancing, the music, the aroma of summer night air, the stars and quarter moon, and the faces and voices of my friends. I asked myself, "How could I have forgotten the joy of being with others and the happiness of belonging to a tribe?" My inner extrovert burst free that night. I was back in the hurly-burly of the world.

From Now On, It's All Gravy

Nobody gets everything, but I have received more than my share of gifts from the universe. I wish everyone could be so fortunate. Friends and strangers often tell me that I am the luckiest person they know. I feel lucky. I am extraordinarily grateful for it. My Princess Cinderella years are over, but many of the blessings of those years remain. As I finish my eighth book, I cannot imagine a life without writing.

My experiences as a public figure have had their costs, but also their great rewards. Overall, I've found the costs more growth-producing than the rewards. The costs are what propelled me to seek peace. But I am grateful for every minute of my life as a writer. Every minute.

Jim isn't perfect, but he is perfect for me. My adult children and grandchildren live nearby and we see each other often. I live in a community of writers, musicians, neighbors, friends and family that I call the Green Boat. (We are traveling together down a swiftly flowing river.) I love my work, which continues to be challenging and endless. Mostly now I do what I like and I like what I do.

Now that I am no longer depressed, I again enjoy meeting people and sharing my ideas. My publishers have been extremely kind to me, and I no longer feel any pressure to endlessly promote my books. I enjoy the limited speaking and teaching that I do. I am grateful to all my old friends for sticking with me, and to my new ones for staying with me now that I am not a front-page story.

Our Siamese cat, Woody, died several years ago, leaving our family "petless." For my sixtieth birthday, I adopted a long-haired calico kitten from the Humane Society. She is just the kind of cat I had wanted as a girl. I named her Glessie, after my father's mother. She stretches beside me as I write in my study and sleeps on my pillow at night. With Glessie around, I laugh more frequently. Every day, I stop my work-oriented life to play or snuggle with her. She is a corrective emotional experience for that puppy in a teacup that I sent away for when I was a girl.

I savor simple pleasures such as a late-afternoon movie, fol-

lowed by a bowl of soup and a glass of wine. Jim and I sit together
with Glessie and talk as we watch Orion turn on the eastern hori-
zon. I am happily ensconced in a landscape that I know and love.
In fact, in many ways, my life is much as it was when I lived in
Beaver City.

My vow is to be grateful. I often think about how many women
have given birth so that I could be here today. How many fathers
have gone hunting and mothers have carried water so that in 1947,
a baby girl named Mary Bray could be born. I am grateful to my
parents for giving me the gift of life; to Grandma Glessie for taking me morel hunting; to my cousin Steve for his lessons on fishing
and kindness; to Grandma Page for giving me books; and to my
aunts for their love and encouragement. I thank all the women
who have cooked me meals, sewed me dresses and tried to teach
me pottery, piano or tap dancing.

I extend my thanks to my bobby-socked school friends and my
old boyfriends. I appreciate my siblings, who lived with me in the
land of childhood and who will be with me as we walk into the
country of old age. I am grateful to my neighbors, friends and Buddhist companions. I am most appreciative of those scampering
healing elixirs that I call my grandchildren. I send blessings to
every grumpy person who has taught me patience and to my many
clients who have taught me about human nature. I am thankful
for all the helpful and creative people who have ever lived. I am
grateful to everyone.

Increasingly, the mail I send and the mail I receive consist of
thank-you notes. At my deepest level, I appreciate that there is an
unseen order and beauty in the universe and that I am part of
unseen perfection. The more I understand that, the more gratitude
I feel.

Like everyone else on the planet, I walk through days of miracles and tragedies. Sorrow and fear, love and peace, are daily as intertwined as smoke and sky. As I grow older, though, my life is filled with more moments of joy. Even when I am in deep pain, I can rescue myself by noticing a small beautiful thing. A golden leaf turning in a cobweb or the smell of a gardenia can stop me in my tracks. Heaven is all around me just waiting for me to notice. As Mary Oliver wrote in her poem "Messenger," "My work is loving the world."

One summer morning, I was up before dawn revising a manuscript. I sat in my old recliner that faces east. When I looked up from my work, I saw the sun rising over the lake. Just beyond our fence, twenty to thirty mallard ducks hunted for bugs in the tall grass. As the nectarine-colored light spread over us, they flew across our fence onto our driveway for a snack of cracked corn. I watched as Duck Number One flew over our fence. She was an ordinary mallard except, this morning, under her wings, a radiant blue light vibrated. The blue was the color of icebergs; only it wasn't a color, really—it was a quality of light. Actually, it was more than light; it was a beacon, a flash of absolute reality. The term "angel wings" came to mind. I was witnessing illuminated light, sparkling blue energy.

I set down the manuscript and watched as duck after duck flew over our fence, all with this radiant blue light-energy flashing. I wanted to wake my husband, but I realized that I could not move. I recalled the phrase "awe-struck" and realized that yes, certain experiences could strike like lightning and leave me immobile.

No doubt scientists could explain the blue energy in terms of the refraction of light in mist under rapidly moving wings. Perhaps I saw neutrinos, those elementary particles that travel close to the speed of light and have no electrical charge. They are said to be a blindingly radiant blue.

However, that would not be the whole story. Was this the light people reported after near-death experiences? Or the throbbing light Moses observed in the Burning Bush? Maybe Ferlin Husky, who sang, "On the wings of a snow-white dove, He sends His pure sweet love," had an experience like mine. Perhaps Hank Williams knew about this rapture when he sang, "I saw the light." What about those lines in "Amazing Grace," "I once was lost, but now I'm found, was blind, but now I see"?

I could write for a month about this experience and never truly capture it. Indeed, religions may have been invented in an effort to explain this beautiful light. Some rituals may be attempts to replicate the conditions that allow us to see this holy light. I experienced the sacred light that people have witnessed in all times and places. It was the most real thing I have ever seen.

At sixty, I am still ahead of the horses, as my grandfather used to say. But I am aware that I have only a finite number left of Thanksgivings, full moons or spring flowers. That realization makes me sad, but it also makes me notice. I don't often squander much time or let beauty pass me by.

I heard recently that Japanese companies offer employees what is called heartache leave—days off after they break up with a partner. With a young person it is only one day; for older people, heartache leave is longer. At this stage of my life, every day is a kind of heartache leave. I am always losing someone or something I love.

But here are the gifts of this stage of life: A deep reverence for all living creatures. The realization I have been useful. The freedom to do as I please. The knowledge that I am loved. The acceptance of my place in time.

I do not fear death, but I hate to think of abandoning people who love me. I wish I could always be here to watch over my generations of family. I especially want to be part of my grandchildren's lives as long as I can. I want to take them to see the Sandhill cranes, read them the books I loved as a girl, teach them the constellations and the names of butterflies. I want to give them what my grandmothers gave me—a deep sense that I was loved and understood.

While my grandchildren have provided meaning in my life, of course they are not my only source of meaning. By now, I have the ten kids I wanted when I was younger, if I count refugees who call me mom, some of my former students and the young people I have helped with their careers. I have my work and my own goals for myself that include reading history and working with people in need.

Not all adults have grandchildren or find them fulfilling. The key to happiness is not so much grandchildren as it is generativity. This was Erik Erikson's term for a sense that our work will leave a good and useful legacy for the generations to come. Many people without children or grandchildren experience this through their professions, their avocations and their commitments to their communities. The fullness of life comes from an identity built on giving and on joy. This is the great trick at this stage in the life cycle—finding useful work that gives us pleasure.

I luxuriate in my life, and it will be hard to say good-bye. Yet death is the greatest democrat. In the end we are all equals. There is a comfort in knowing that I face what every human being who has ever lived faced in his or her time. I expect to return to the great commons where all our ancestors will be waiting to greet us. I predict that whatever comes after death will be better than I can possibly imagine.

In sixty years of living, my knowledge has increased and my taste has become more sophisticated, but my values have not changed much at all. My greatest faith has always been in kindness. My mother educated me in that lesson, and the Dalai Lama has given me a refresher course.

My questions about *my* life are all of our eternal questions: How can we best develop our gifts and use them to help others? How can we keep growing until we stop breathing? How can we stay present? How can we be happy? The answers are universal answers: Pay attention, tell the truth, be kind, and find things to appreciate and enjoy every day. Try to learn something from everyone. Be open to wonder. As I read this list, I realize my mother or grandmother could have written it. Perhaps this is what most humans discover by the time their hair turns silver.

All transformations are returns. After setting forth on a voyage of discovery, being chased by monsters, encountering great suffering and beauty, getting lost and being pummeled by storms, we find our way back to our original place and realize that the truth has always been there waiting for us. We connect with that which we knew before we were born. We can resume our ordinary lives with eyes unclouded by longing.

MY BIRTHDAY PARTY

Late Friday afternoon, Jim and I and Sara and her husband, John, pile into our Honda to drive ninety miles to my son's town to celebrate my birthday. This is not an ordinary party with a cake and a few small gifts. Because it is my decade birthday, I have taken the liberty of asking for what I really want—gifts involving creativity and self-expression. I cannot wait to see what the evening brings.

As we cruise down the interstate toward the sunset, the golden leaves of the cottonwoods and the tall grasses wave to us. We speak of global warming, the Blackwater scandals and the possibility of war with Iran. When we turn off onto a small highway that meanders north to my son's town, John smiles and says, "The topics will change soon."

When we arrive, six-year-old Kate is pacing up and down the sidewalk. She is no longer my cuddly baby but a tall girl with long chestnut hair and wonky glasses. She still likes to sit on our laps, but as my son put it, "Holding Kate is like holding a baby giraffe."

Shouting "Happy Birthday," she jumps into the car to hug me.

Four-year-old A.B. rushes down the steps barefoot and, as usual, superglues himself to my side. While the others carry in cameras and guitars, I snuggle with him and with Claire Annelise, who has butter-colored pigtails on top of her head.

In the steamy, aromatic kitchen, my handsome son is sweating as he stirs big pots of lamb tikka Madras and cinnamon-flavored rice. Already, platters of tandoori shrimp and grilled pineapple cover the counters. Zeke says, "Mom, this is my act of creativity. I am preparing the best meal I've ever made to show you my love."

As I watch Zeke work, I think of my father, who cooked lavish meals for guests in our red-tiled kitchen in Beaver City. I picture my brother Jake, in his crowded San Francisco apartment, preparing the exotic and complicated dishes that my family favors. I see myself, for the last forty years, baking rum cakes, making chipped beef gravy on toast and stirring stroganoff.

I ask Zeke if I can give A.B. a few predinner shrimp, and he says, "It's your birthday. You can do whatever you want." I hold my grandson on my lap and pat his thick, curly hair so like my father's and mine. I hand him shrimp after shrimp. As he gobbles them down, I think of the shrimp my dad bought by the bucket in Mexico in the 1950s and the shrimp cocktails my mother served at Thanksgiving dinner in Kansas. For at least fifty years, shrimp has been the coin of our realm.

We dine around Jamie's big oak table set with her best china. A.B. says grace. "Thank you, God, for giving me a great Nonna." Amen, I breathe. Amen.

We pass the naan and raita and laugh as we praise the food and each other. For dessert, we have pies. As a girl, my favorite dessert was my mother's pecan pie. For thirty years, my friend Jan has baked me a pecan pie on my birthday. Tonight she has sent a cherry raspberry pie along with the pecan. Almost everyone wants a sliver of both, and soon Claire is covered in raspberries.

After dinner, we move into the living room for gifts. I sit on the couch with John on one side, Zeke on the other, and A.B. on my lap. Kate presents me with several beautiful drawings and a sheet of paper covered with "I love Nonna" in many colors. Not surprisingly, A.B. has lost the drawing he made for me. He is like his father was at his age, scattered and inclined to misplace things. But he hands me a couple of last-minute artworks. Next, the three kids line up and recite Christina Rossetti's poem "Caterpillar." Even little Claire knows it by heart.

This recitation reminds me of Grandpa Page, who entertained us after dinner by reciting his own poems and those of others. I can picture my bald grandpa dressed in a white shirt and overalls in the small living room in Flagler. He would recite by heart Robert Service poems such as "The Cremation of Sam McGee," or his own poems such as "The Mother of My Babies."

Kate has written a play starring herself, her mom, A.B. and Claire. Her plot is that a boy comes to a new school and is nervous and lonely. A kind girl befriends him and helps him adjust. My daughter-in-law, Jamie, reads the introduction, then A.B. happily shouts out his lines. When it is Kate's turn to speak, she freezes. She wants to call off the play and wails, "I can't do this." Her parents work with her for a while. Jamie says, "You'll feel bad tomorrow if you don't do this, Kate." Zeke suggests, "Come sit on my lap and deliver your lines from here." In her father's arms, Kate thaws out and recites her lines. I appreciate how much courage it takes her to carry on after a failure of nerve.

Somehow, my daughter-in-law, who is a mother, a teacher and

a pastor's wife, has carved out the time to make me beautiful gifts. Jamie hands me notecards she has crafted with brown paper and decorated with wild grasses. She presents me with framed photos of my grandchildren's eyes. How different each pair is in shape, how exactly the same in blueness and clarity!

With eyes more than any other feature, it is Pete and Repeat across the generations. Kate has the heavy-lidded eyes of my father, my cousin Junior and my son. A.B.'s eyes express the depth of his soul in a way that reminds me of my mother's and my brother John's. Claire's eyes contain the mischief of my aunt Henrietta and my sister, Toni.

Next it is Sara's turn to present me with her gift. She is a creative writer who works in communications at the university. Two years ago, she gave us the gift of moving from Washington, D.C., back to Nebraska to live near our family. Ten years ago, she wrote me a poem titled "To My Mother on My Twentieth Birthday." Tonight she has written me this poem, which she reads in her strong voice.

For My Mama on Her Sixtieth

I.

There's a thing she does, uniquely her.
Zeke calls it going meta, to me it is
clicking over . . . a turning
and then suddenly she's not a middle-aged Nebraska mother,
she is a Buddha, explaining the nature of things

as she sees it

unfolding out her favorite window,

unfurling over a frozen lake,

a blanket of winter grass.

II.

She likes to read books about Sierra Leone,

Rwanda, Burma. Any civil conflict will do.

Water rights, dead presidents, dusty old women who did

    extraordinary things when

they were young and beautiful—or plain—who now live only in

    the stained pages

of books left dormant on library bookshelves 51 weeks a year.

She likes Abe Lincoln and Shelby Foote and LBJ,

stories of dust bowls and blizzards and shipwrecks,

sympathizes with Marie Antoinette—she was a woman of her

    times, after all—and Anne Boleyn.

Once, she spent her Saturday night watching a documentary about a

    tree.

Even the most devoted daughter

can't fabricate a detail like that.

III.

C'mere, Lucy. Ooooooooh, who's my little granddog?

Who's my sweet girl?

Do you love your Nonna?

Would you like a snack? Do you want to go for a walk?
Oooooooh, you love your Nonna, don't you?

IV.

Here are things she used to cook for me:
Sukiyaki, bulkogi, slivers of yellow daikon that glowed like neon.
Polenta. Ratatouille.
Herring and gefilte fish and pickled tongue.
Oh, my!
Cilantro at Christmas? NO-el.
She redeemed herself a decade later, however, by brashly declaring
rosemary
the spice of the nineties.

V.

She keeps getting smaller.
Her arms and legs more birdlike,
a comparison she would favor, probably.
Since the birds are her constants,
here a nuthatch, there a redwing.
Everywhere a grackle grackle.
"Look, Norman, the loons are back!"
Maybe they follow her, this thin woman who circles the lake,
her own daily migration.
Maybe they think she will lead them home.

By the time she is finished, I am crying. I praise her poem, but inside myself, I am praising something deeper. Sara makes me "feel felt." We understand each other so well. We will be connected until I die and even after I die, just as I am still connected to my mother.

Jim reads a poem he has written, a poem filled with family in-jokes called "Thirteen Things Not to Tell Mary on Her Sixtieth Birthday." We laugh and applaud and then for a minute we are quiet. Relishing. What a lovely program this has been, with the children bouncing between us, my three big guys nearby and Jamie and Sara showering me with smiles. Since I arrived in this small Nebraska town along the Platte, I have felt wrapped in a warm blanket.

Jim announces that the grand finale will be music in the dining room. He and John quickly set up equipment and tune their guitars. Jim plays lead guitar while John plays the bass that Jim gave him for a wedding present. Jamie, Kate and Sara gather around them to sing. A.B. and Claire volunteer to be the dancers. They stand at the ready in the small space between the table and Zeke and me, the only audience members. We two sit side by side holding hands.

The family band breaks into one of my favorite songs, Stephen Foster's "Hard Times Come Again No More." Jim sings the first verse in his strong, deep voice. This steady, kind man has been with me through graduate school, the rearing of our children, the death of all of our parents, my years of success as an author and my emotional crash. Through it all, he has played music and made me laugh.

Kate, Sara and Jamie join him on the chorus. Claire turns circles as she waves her arms in the air over her pigtails. A.B. dances with a variety of jumps and cool moves that he worked out at Sara's wedding a month earlier. All of my grandchildren appear to have inherited my father's exuberance and my parents' energy. By the second verse, Zeke and I are crying. We share the same soul and understand the world in much the same way. We both know that there are many more people in the room than we can see.

When Jamie was a girl, she sang at weddings and funerals in her hometown in the Sandhills. Now she sings for me in her lovely, lyrical voice. With her long, dark hair swinging behind her, she sways to the music and beams at me. I turn my attention to good-looking, shaved-headed John who concentrates on his playing. He is new to our family and yet already a part of us. With his warm heart and generosity, he is as likable as Grandma Glessie or my cousin Steve.

I determine I will memorize every moment of this evening. I want to hold this night forever in the same way I held that night long ago fishing with my father. Sara sings the last verse in her beautiful alto voice. Both she and Jamie could have been singers, and perhaps they still will be. I hope they have sixty years of new experiences in front of them.

Zeke and I are the long-term members of this family. He was here before Jim or Sara, or any of the others. We created this room filled with kin. Now we weep together at the poignancy of the song. Even as the lyrics plead for no more hard times, we all know they will come again. Zeke also cries because I am getting older and he will miss me one day.

Time is both lovely and terrible. It gave me my grandparents and it took them away. It offered me lively young parents and broken old ones. Time allowed me a childhood in a quiet, rural place and catapulted me into airports, green rooms and auditoriums. It gave me what my grandmother called "bright eyes" and my less-than-perfect eyes of today. The early 1970s brought me a long-haired rock-and-roll singer, and in 2007, he is still with me, although now he wears glasses and watches his cholesterol. To-night, time delivers to me her greatest gift—Jim, these beautiful children and grandchildren singing together on a dark Nebraska evening.

As I observe our family band, I do not see individuals sepa-rate and complete in themselves. Rather, I see a kaleidoscope of colorful bits from multiple generations of family. I see the glitter of character, movement, facial expression and emotional essence. We all share the amber love of birds and the natural world. We carry a ruby-colored fascination with people and an opalescent love of story.

We are here tonight because, since the beginning of the human race, certain people have made love to certain people. Our bodies are built from Grandma Glessie's fried perch, Aunt Agnes's creamed corn and Aunt Grace's biscuits and gravy. The long backbones of my father and brothers now live on in the frame of my grandson. My mother's slender fingers wave from Claire's little hands. Aunt Margaret's liveliness and curiosity radiate from my children and grandchildren. Everyone in this room is "green on top."

Grandmother Page's character glows around Kate, who is kind to every living creature. In Claire, I see my mother's particular set of chin and jaw. In my daughter and son, I see the emerald of my grandmother Glessie's powerful presence. They carry the family grit of insomnia and the sapphires of eagerness to help the world. The jewels of this kaleidoscope swirl before me, faster and faster, until the scene is simply a blur of sparkly light.

This room is no longer a room. We have stopped time and moved outside of space. We are deep into something beyond poetry, beyond even breathing. We are nestled in the womb of time, where all walls are made of love. Long after everyone in this room has crossed over, our DNA will continue to swirl in new bodies. Our eyes will shine in new faces. The party will go on.

I am back to where I began my journey sixty years ago in the Ozarks. I can hear the universe singing to me, "You are loved. You are safe." All my life I have waited for this moment and now it is here.

ACKNOWLEDGMENTS

Thanks to my readers—Jane Isay, Sara Pipher, Jim Pipher, Jamie Pipher, Jan Zegers, Pam Barger, Lynda Madison, and Dave Myers, and to my writers' group, Prairie Trout.

Thanks to my friends and family and to those who helped me with this book—Beatty Brasch, Kim Beyer-Nelson, Jim Cole, Kitty Fynbu, John Gilliam, Cindy Hischke, Mohamed Jalloh, Dixie and Fred Lubin, Heidi Piccini, Zeke Pipher, Ardis Prochnow, Margaret Rickers, Chris and Cathy Sayre, Janice Spellerberg, Jan Stenberg, the Unitarian Church of Lincoln, Laura Wertz, Pauline Zande, Angela Zegers and the Zen Center of Omaha.

I want to express my deepest respect and appreciation for my editor, Jake Morrissey, who worked brilliantly and tirelessly on this manuscript. I am grateful for Sarah Bowlin's kind and efficient assistance. Thanks to my publicists and friends, Mih-Ho Cha and Marilyn Ducksworth, for their loyalty and competence over these many years, and welcome aboard to my new publicist, Claire

McGinnis. I thank also my publishers, Geoffrey Kloske and Susan Petersen Kennedy.

I want to offer my agent, Susan Lee Cohen, special kudos. She has been with me since the beginning and has never failed to offer kind, sensible and ethical advice.

Mary Pipher, Ph.D., is a psychologist and the author of eight books, including the *New York Times* bestsellers *Reviving Ophelia, The Shelter of Each Other*, and *Another Country*, as well as *Writing to Change the World*. Her work has been translated into more than twenty-five languages, and she has lectured to groups and conferences around the world. Visit her website at www.marypipher.net.

P.O. 0005333856 20230519